$\mathcal{P}$oetry Comes Up Where It Can

AN ANTHOLOGY

The Amicus Journal is a publication of the Natural Resources Defense Council (NRDC), a national nonprofit organization founded in 1970 and dedicated to protecting the world's natural resources and ensuring a safe and healthy environment for all people. With 400,000 members and a staff of lawyers, scientists, and other environmental specialists, NRDC combines the power of law, the power of science, and the power of people in defense of the environment. *Amicus* (ə mē' kəs) is Latin for "friend." Its most common usage is in the phrase *amicus curiae*, which means "friend of the court," a role NRDC has played on many occasions as an advocate for the environment.

POEMS FROM *THE AMICUS JOURNAL*, 1990–2000

*P*oetry Comes Up Where It Can

AN ANTHOLOGY

EDITED BY Brian Swann

FOREWORD BY Mary Oliver

THE UNIVERSITY OF UTAH PRESS   Salt Lake City, Utah

Art by Maureen O'Hara Ure

The poems in this anthology originally appeared in *The Amicus Journal*.
For permission to reprint them, grateful acknowledgment is made to each
author. Further acknowledgment is made to the holders of copyright and
publishers of the following poems:

ACKNOWLEDGMENTS

Mary Oliver. "At the Shore," "Snapshots," published as "Sand Dabs, Three," and
"Poem 12 from 'West Wind,'" from *West Wind*, copyright 1997 by Mary Oliver,
reprinted by permission of Houghton Mifflin Company. "Rice," from *New and
Selected Poems*, copyright 1992 by Mary Oliver, reprinted by permission of Beacon
Press, Boston. "The Lark's Nest" and "Design," copyright 1991 by Mary Oliver;
"The Fox," copyright 1993 by Mary Oliver; and "Waking on a Summer Morning,"
copyright 1999 by Mary Oliver; all reprinted by permission of the Molly Malone
Cook Literary Agency.

Michael Dorris. "Prey," copyright 1991 by Michael Dorris, reprinted by permission
of Charles Rembar for the Michael Dorris Estate.

William Heyen. "Emancipation Proclamation," from *Pterodactyl Rose: Poems of
Ecology*, copyright 1991 by Time Being Press.

Duane Niatum. "Rufous Hummingbird" and "The Salmon," from *The Crooked
Beak of Love*, copyright by Duane Niatum, reprinted courtesy of West End Press.

Pattiann Rogers. "Opus from Space," "The Kingdom of Heaven," and "Into the
Light," from *Eating Bread and Honey* (Milkweed Editions, 1997), copyright Pattiann
Rogers.

William Stafford. "Gulls at Cannon Beach" reprinted by permission of the Estate of
William Stafford.

LIBRARY OF CONGRESS CATALOGING-IN-PUBLICATION DATA

Poetry comes up where it can : an anthology : poems from the Amicus
journal, 1900–2000 / edited by Brian Swann ; foreword by Mary Oliver.
   p. cm.
  ISBN 0-87480-644-5 (alk. paper)
  1. Nature—Poetry—20th century. I. Swann, Brian.

PS595.N22 P636 2000
811'.5408—dc21   99-051678

CONTENTS

FOREWORD

I.

THIS COLLECTION OF poems from the magazine *Amicus*, from a
breadth of serious and glad voices, contains a serene richness. It is
certainly a book for those of us who love nature, are devout con-
cerning nature, and get out into it whenever we can. And it is a
book for young readers who, urban or country raised, are probably
more familiar these days with the confessional poem, or the therapy
poem, than with the poem of Otherness. It is for older readers who
are perhaps forced to shorter walks and to finding their natural
world as much in recollection as in new adventures. And it is, also,
for those readers who do not think and dream leaves and rivers all
day long. Maybe, in fact, it is especially for them.

In any audience there are two kinds of listeners. The first are
relaxed and anticipatory because they have prior knowledge of the
material and belief in its merit. The other sort, who have just wan-
dered by, let us say, and now casually find themselves picking up
and opening a book whose premise and examples they are either
strangers to or have, so far, resisted, are also welcome here. Let the
doors to the temple be always open!

This foreword is a narrative, or course. It is also a persuasion.

2.

As we move to the end of the century we begin to see our immedi-
ate past in its fascinating and complex entirety. It is not altogether a
shining thing that we see. Undoubtedly it has been humankind's
most inventive, most intelligent, and most compassionate century.
Also the bloodiest, the most destructive. What we have destroyed
was, in part, ideas. But ideas are forever rising and collapsing; it is
in their nature, in fact, to rise and thrive and then fall—to give birth
to the next. Other kinds of devastation are not so affirmative.
During this hundred-year parcel of time the landscapes of our world
have been literally torn apart, and what was, is gone forever. You
may say that this too has been happening for millennia, and you

would not be wrong. The original forests of Europe, and the clear-running Mississippi, and the free-flowing Colorado, and the lush green island called Manhattan have been gone for a long time. But, hear this: gone now, in this century, is the last square mile of earth or sea that had not yet been touched by some excruciation or taint of our own making.

Previously there appeared such depth and abundance of everything around us that, whatever the forces of usage and change, it did not seem a matter for concern, or even serious thought. But now we have looked into the future, and we can see ahead of us: a dry, cold, dark, voiceless planet. Such is the possible future of everything, including ourselves. And the mystery, the mystery of all of it, of our lives and the lives of thrushes and wasps and clouds and the burning-bright tiger is not yet even begun to be understood! Such a thought should freeze the heart in its tracks.

3.

But: enough. We have all heard the hard facts and the terrifying pre-ordinations. What I want to talk about is love. For truth by itself is enfeebled; it is *merely the truth*; it is without force unless the heart's desire is there too. Moreover my statements have already been too simple. As we cannot talk about human need and human progress and leave out the trees and the rivers, neither can we speak on behalf of wilderness and leave out hunger, disease, or other human misery. Long and complicated are the discussions that will bring help and health to everyone, and everything. But this I believe with all my heart: we must love not only each other, we must love our world. We must love the robin that sings in the green shade of the maple; the little monkey with the golden mantle, goblin of the rainforest; the banks of red roses flourishing on the pale dunes of the Province-lands; and even the beetle shining in the cup of the single rose.

We are children and kin not only of each other but of the earth and the sky. The yardstick and the telescope, and the laser and the vaccines have altered our world and our lives. But there is still, in each of us, recognized or not, a desire and a need for bonding with the universe. It is this reaching out toward the nonhuman—the utlimate, the mystery—that can make of our brief lives something not only successful and cheerful and interesting but—I do not whisper the word but say it boldly—divine.

4.

Nature as it exists around us and as it exists in the mind has, over and over, since poetical and philosophical thought began, been interpreted in this way. Nature is not without destructive force, but it is without malice. It does not operate without nurturing and protecting in the context of self-interest, but it does so without greed. It has no ambition except to exist; it has a capacity for joyfulness, for idling, for refining the useful song into cadences of lyrical excess. It is an endless, rich invitation. Give Emerson a starry sky, and he is off on discussions of universe and spirit that, in the mind, swing open a hundred doors. Give Turner a cloudscape, and he will swirl the paints into a remembrance of the moment that the eye can swim into a century away. Give a child a week in the northwoods of Maine, and she will come home washed in the rains of radiance. There is a fever that natural beauty imparts that goes by many names: gratitude, devotion, clarity, humility, astonishment, grace. Without doubt, when we do violence to the earth we are doing violence to our own lives as well.

5.

So, then, if the truths and the cautions will not keep us from rash behaviors, can not instill in us the necessary respect for this Otherness, what will?

The answer, in part at least, is: pleasure. What we enjoy, we value. What we feel is making our lives richer and more meaningful, we cherish. And what we cherish, we will defend. Said William Blake—not really asking but telling—"Are not religion and politics the same thing?"

6.

Of course, we cannot love what we have not noticed.

7.

A poem, in and of itself, is as musical and full of pictorial force as a long walk on a summer day. It offers pleasure through its innate structure—its rhythms, illustrations, ideas, suggestions—and also by its invitational demeanor. A poem is, indeed, less important as a literary achievement than as a passage between the world—Otherness —and the solitary mind. It wishes to bring the reader to awareness and thought—two powerful agents of change. When we read poems about nature, we ourselves, through the transparencies of their careful construction and through the craft of the imagination, are able to reach beyond ourselves. We exist, for a moment, in the instance of the poem. One of the miracles of Shelley is precisely this gift. How willingly he urges each of us to stand in the field and hear the skylark for ourselves! In his musicality and his wisdom, in his invisibility, how he suggests thought after thought until they feel, profoundly and intimately, like our own! And so, in a poem almost two hundred years old, through the generosity of a poet who knew that the important thing was not the story but the experiencing of the story, each of us can begin or deepen our own journey into the leaves and the sky—into an attitude of noticing.

THERE ARE A MULTITUDE of such generous poems in the present collection. They all have marvelous stories to tell, though the events that they talk about are not necessarily rare or death-defying, not at all. The stories are wonderful because they are wrapped in serenity and because they are as fresh with caring and respect as the first white mist rising in the morning like a veil off the shining river. Every one of them is written in love and earnestness, in the hope that hearts will change.

How heavy and alone we often feel in the place our kind has carved for itself! But there are other ways to live. As Denise Levertov wrote while watching the little wren that, in spite of her presence, went on with its beautiful life,

> I feel myself lifted,
> lightened, dispersed:
>
> it has turned me to air, . . .

Mary Oliver

PREFACE

THE "TWO CULTURES" battle C. P. Snow wrote about over thirty years ago is still with us, and from time to time I still get asked: Why is there poetry in *Amicus*, a journal published by the Natural Resources Defense Council (NRDC), an organization devoted to the nation's environmental regulatory systems, both legal and scientific? In reply, I say only that poetry sprouts everywhere; you can't stop it. It has been growing in the pages of *Amicus* from its founding over a quarter of a century ago, nurtured by the first editor, Peter Borrelli. It continued in those of his successor, Francesca Lyman, and in her successor, the present editor, Kathrin Day Lassila. Poetry even finds its way into official documents at NRDC. In "A Force of Nature," a retrospective for NRDC's twenty-fifth anniversary, the pages are leavened and enlivened with poems by Linda Hogan, W. S. Merwin, Mary Oliver, Wendell Berry, Denise Levertov, and John Haines.

Clearly, at NRDC poetry interprets the world in ways complementary to science and law. It takes us into the deeper reasons why we bother about the land, the Earth. Poetry's emotional resonances remind us why we care. And poetry fits neatly into NRDC's statement of purpose, which reads, in part: "Ultimately, NRDC strives to help create a new way of life for humankind—one that can be sustained indefinitely without fouling or depleting the resources that support all life on Earth." It's not too much of a stretch to include poetry among these resources, to consider poetry integral to the new way of life, since it is vital to our being, affirming and defining, discriminating, integrating, revealing, renewing and opening up, giving thanks. It conserves the best that we are and suggests ways to be better. It says what must be said in the best ways possible, and in the process can itself be sustained indefinitely with the right kind of care and attention.

Amicus publishes fewer than twenty poems a year, a very small percentage of those we receive for consideration. Doubtless, the present selection has a certain editorial slant or bias; by derivation, an "anthology" is only a handful of flowers. But I like to think there is some variety here, from satire and humor to celebration and paean. There are many well-known poets, but there are also poets who are just starting out.

I would like to thank many people who have helped in the creation of this book, from my editor at the University of Utah Press, Glenda Cotter, and the director, Jeffrey Grathwohl, to the *Amicus* staff of Peggy Alevrontas, Dana Nadel Foley, and Kathrin Day Lassila. I am especially grateful to Dana and Kathrin for their unfailing and generous support, friendship, and editorial acumen. I would also like to take this opportunity to thank the original founders and organizers of NRDC for all their energy and vision, and the current board and staff for all the important work they continu to do. In particular, I'd like to thank NRDC's long-time leader, John Adams. Without NRDC there would be no *Amicus*! Finally, I want to thank all the poets in this volume, not only for their wonderful poems but also for donating their royalties to NRDC's lawsuit to remedy extreme mercury poisoning in Maine's Penobscot River, just as their predecessors in *Poetry From the Amicus Journal* (Tioga Publishing Company, 1990) donated their royalties to NRDC's litiga-tion against Exxon for the "Exxon Valdez" disaster.

Brian Swann
Poetry Editor, *The Amicus Journal*

NOTE

In my inaugural editor's note of 1994, I wrote, "*Amicus* exists to seek out the most critical emerging events and the most interesting new ideas, and hold them up to the light in original, searching prose. It also aspires to convey . . . the emotional and spiritual wellsprings of environmental commitment." That was an ambitious, not to say audacious, goal; *Amicus* yearns after it with every issue. But part of what allowed me to declare it publicly was the knowledge that the poetry in *Amicus* will always elevate us to the level of great reading. Everyone who mentions the poems to me says or implies the same thing: that Brian's bone-true feeling for verse gives us poems that ring in the ear and heart for days if not years after first reading. For this, and for his hard work, delightful friendship, and humor, no thanks is sufficient for Brian.

Brian has thanked many of those responsible for *Amicus* already, but let me reiterate some of his kudos: to the *Amicus* staff, Peggy Alevrontas, Dana Nadel Foley, and designer Nancy Butkus, all of them made of iron and talent; to our dedicated and inspiring editorial board, particularly Joan K. Davidson, Philip B. Korsant, John B. Oakes, and the board's brilliant chairman, Jonathan Z. Larsen; and to John Adams and Frances Beinecke, president and executive director of NRDC. It was John who first conceived the idea of a magazine that would be the "flagship of the environmental movement." Together, he and Frances lead and sustain an extraordinary organization, and *Amicus* is proud to be published by it.

Kathrin Day Lassila
Editor, *The Amicus Journal*

Poetry Comes Up Where It Can

An Anthology

Antler

⌒ STAR-STRUCK UTOPIAS OF 2000

What if Society became so obsessed with the stars
    as a result of Emerson's epiphany
"If the stars came out only one night in a thousand years
    how people would believe and adore
        and preserve from generation to generation
    remembrance of the miracle they'd been shown"
That everyone started sleeping during the day
    so they could stay up all night
        star-gazing, star-thinking, star-dreaming,
Being in the Milky Way so they could have
    maximum exposure to the Universe
        beyond Earth and our own Star.
Rather than being consumed by human history,
    art, literature, music, religion, politics, business,
        consumed by the stars, hunger
    to be with them and
        star-roving MilkyWaydom,
So much so that people spent more time
    looking at the Milky Way than at each other,
        more time looking up
    than straight ahead or down.
Total blackout in all cities—
    no streetlights, stoplights, carlights,
        driving at night illegal,
    no lights in buildings but candles,
Whole populations thronging to darkened
    baseball stadiums and skyscrapertops
        to sit holding hands en masse
    and look up at the billion year spree
        of the realm of the nebulae!

Breathing air with snow falling through it
   thinking how flour is sifted through a sieve
Each different snowflake design is a sieve
   and the air is charged with the energy
      of each snowflake design
       falling through it,
Air passing through the shapes
   of openings in the interior
    of each falling flake
   as well as along the edges,
Serrating in minute invisible architectures
   zillion-shaped clarified vibrancy
      of snowflake sculpture reality
    the edges of snowflake symmetry
     chiseling microscopically
    into an invisible display
      of snowflake-sculptured air
    beyond human comprehension.
And as an animal leaves its track
   in wet sand or mud
     so each snowflake design
   leaves its track
    in cool moist air
   as it falls,
So that in breathing air
   snowflakes have passed through
     you breathe the invisible tracks
   their designs have imprinted
    in the air

And as a hunter follows the bear
   by stepping in its tracks
     you follow the snow
   by breathing the invisible
     patterns of its designs
        pressed into the air
     as it falls.

Alison Apotheker

❧ BURNING BUSH (*Dictamnus Albus*)

I would like to believe that in the darkness
beneath the skin, the secret dark holds
the same volatile oil as these flowers
and will ignite the stricken
silence of this summer night.

And I would like to believe the soul's
language resides there, and the unfinished phrases
of the dead ones, the ellipsis completed
in a crush of those dark green toothed
leaves and their scent of sliced lemon.

I would hope as well that the lightning
in its body finds rest beneath the soil
and knows, as sure as the capillaries
whisper of blood's persistent passage,
that all will be remembered and spoken for.

Homero Aridjis

ෆ BORDERS, CAGES AND WALLS

We pin dates to shadows,
wire-in the present.
Shut a body into a schedule,
into brick birdcages.
We put shoes on the imagination,
shirt and pants on the open air.
We narrow the outlook,
haul in the passions with our nets.
Manacle the hands,
and blinker the eyes, shrink
the sunbeams down to size.

Life keeps its distance,
love holds its tongue,
and poetry comes up where it can.

Translated by George McWhirter

The nature of a river is to run
and its verb: to flow.
They have poured down from the sky,
the rain and the hills.
Their currents swollen with toads and blood, willows and thirst.
Some were spawned in love beds
by mortal women,
giving birth to clans and champions
and dry everyday men
who carry them in their names.
They are portrayed as a green body,
legs entwined and arms spread wide,
a changeable mirror that reflects an eye
of fresh water that eddies swiftly away.
For the people's adorations
a small altar is their due —not a temple,
oxen and horses thrown in for sacrifice,
a maiden garbed in the raiment of a goddess
with a yellow face.

Before, sparkling rivers ran
through this green valley:
ash grey, chestnut and opaline; lost,
and wandering, purple and dull brown,
squalling and clamouring
down from the steaming mountain
onto the lazy plain
touching on early Tenochtitlan.
Today they groan, thick with black water
and crawling with crap, shrunk into conduits,

ridiculous rivers without banks —their docked tails
reined into lanes raging with cars, hurtling
down through the deflowered city,
reaching their mouth in lethal lakes
and the scarred sea that no longer loves them.

Translated by George McWhirter

Denise Y. Arnold

✍ Song to the Alpaca

Apaq	Bring her down,
apaqmay,	bring her down,
Warawar michanti . . .	With the lamp of the stars . . .
Ichuq	Carry her down,
ichuqmay,	carry her down in your arms,
Chullumpi	Diver-bird
Apaq	Bring her down,
apaqmay,	bring her down,
Chullumpi	Diver-bird
Warawar ninanti . . .	With the fire of the stars . . .
Wayñurarapikitalla	Please sing it just for me
Wa wiya way chullumpi	Going the way of the diver-bird
T"uqurarapikitalla	Please dance it just for me
Wa wiya way chullumpi . . .	Going the way of the diver-bird
. . . pantis t'ik"itay . . .	. . . crimson-flowered just the same
Warawar michanti	With the light of the stars
Ichuq	Bring her down,
ichuqmay	bring her down in your arms
Rusas t'ik"itay . . .	rose-flowered just the same

From a song by Doña María Ayka Llanque
Recorded and translated by Denise Y. Arnold
and Juan de Dios Yapita

Robin Becker

How neatly this world divides
in half after sunset in Wyoming.

All the loneliness
sinks below the plush, dark

silhouette of buttes and cottonwoods.
Into the huge, light sky rises

hope, our best intentions,
tomorrow's weather.

Ted Benttinen

✒ MARITIME PASTORAL

The feathered discs of asters trace
the lower sun, stars following a star.
Yellow and purple, the colors of resurrection,
are out of season. A green heron,
hunchbacked and solitary among the reeds,
stalks the panicked killifish.
Tropical air is streaming northward—
Caribbean salt mixes with the falling fires
of maple and scrub oak. The white and pink petals
of salt-spray roses fall, exposing the red hips.
Black skimmers etch the glass of a salt pond,
snapping at juvenile alewives.
The miniature trees of sea lavender are blooming,
and the flowers of thrift fulfill their other name.
On the outer bar, there is a subtle shift of pattern—
the swell veers southeast, lengthens,
sends a warning into the hulls of trawlers.

Bruce Berger

♂ PHOTO SAFARI

I get them in range and shoot.
The beasts I bead on linger
To leap in another sight.
I hunt from a different hunger.

My quarry shoots back. Its light
Hammers an animal
That blooms in second sight,
An icon on my wall

Whose flesh is food for the eyes.
Like any civilized case
I only collect my prize
In scrip, and after the race.

So I mint for the inner eye
As reformed assassins must.
Cocking my conscience, I
Discharge with a joy that's just

And bring back the breath inert.
Hunter as hypocrite?
Surrogate murder as art?
If there's a future, that's it.

Wendell Berry

ℰ **G**ETTING **A**WAY: **V**ERSES AND **C**HORUSES FOR **V**ARIOUS **V**OICES

Oh, when the sky is choked with smoke
And knives and pistols rule the night,
Then get away, let's get away
To where the stars are shining bright.

It is a problem, we confess,
And the true measure of our success,
That every way that we progress,
Making money, we make a mess.

The slums are overflowing
With invaders from the sticks.
The streets are all a-crawling
With multi-colored hicks.

[*Chorus*]

Then buy a mobile home;
Put sorrow on the road.
The Interstate will help you
To bear your heavy load.

[*Chorus*]

You will live then like Daniel Boone
Where every star is shining bright
On color TV in your RV
In a new campground every night.

[*Chorus*]

Or move out in the country,
For the country's so genteel,

And all the country people
Feel the way real people feel.

Having achieved success,
We're changing our address
As upward we progress
From mess to mess to mess.

And when the country people
Have lost their wit and charm,
It's time then to uncouple
And subdivide the farm.

[*Chorus*]

We'll make our way in haste
To the wilds of Outer Space
Where people of good taste
Escape the human race.

[*Chorus*]

But Outer Space sucks up our cash
To our intense exasperation,
And it is littered with the trash
Of international cooperation.

We ride away and ride away
Upon the wave of our success
Only to find that we've escaped
Into somebody else's mess.

But making a mess is fine (okay?)
So long as we can get away.

✑ LET US PLEDGE

Let us pledge allegiance to the flag
and to the national sacrifice areas
for which it stands, garbage dumps
and empty holes, sold out for a higher
spire on the rich church, the safety
of voyagers in golf carts, the better mood
of the stock market. Let us feast
today, though tomorrow we starve. Let us
gorge upon the body of the Lord, consuming
the earth for our greater joy in Heaven,
that fair Vacationland. Let us wander forever
in the labyrinths of our self-esteem.
Let us evolve forever toward the higher
consciousness of the machine.
The spool of our engine-driven fate
unwinds, our history now outspeeding
thought, and the heart is a beatable tool.

The Mad Farmer, Flying the Flag of Rough Branch, Secedes from the Union

From the union of power and money,
from the union of power and secrecy,
from the union of government and science,
from the union of government and art,
from the union of science and money,
from the union of ambition and ignorance,
from the union of genius and war,
from the union of outer space and inner vacuity,
the Mad Farmer walks quietly away.

There is only one of him, but he goes.
He returns to the small country he calls home,
his own nation small enough to walk across.
He goes shadowy into the local woods,
and brightly into the local meadows and croplands.
He goes to the care of neighbors,
he goes into the care of neighbors.
He goes to the potluck supper, a dish
from each house for the pleasure of every house.
He goes into the quiet of early mornings
of days when he is not going anywhere.

Calling his neighbors together into the sanctity
of their lives separate and together
in the one life of their commonwealth and home,
in their own nation small enough for a story
or song to travel across in an hour, he cries:

Come all ye conservatives and liberals
who want to conserve the good things and be free,

come away from the merchants with big answers,
whose hands are metalled with power;
from the union of anywhere and everywhere
by the purchase of everything from everybody at the lowest price
and the sale of anything to anybody at the highest price;
from the union of work and debt, work and despair;
from the wage-slavery of the helplessly well-employed.

From the union of self-gratification and self-annihilation,
from the union of solution and pollution,
secede into care for one another
and for the good gifts of Heaven and Earth.

Come into the life of the body, the one body
granted to you in all the history of time.
Come into the body's economy, its daily work,
and its replenishment at mealtimes and at night.
Come into the body's thanksgiving, when it knows
and acknowledges itself a living soul.
Come into the dance of the community, joined
in a circle, hand in hand, the dance of the eternal
love of women and men for one another
and of neighbors and friends for one another.

Always disappearing, always returning,
calling his neighbors to return, to think again
of the care of flocks and herds, of gardens
and fields, of woodlot and forest and the untouched groves,
calling them separately and together, calling and calling,
he goes forever toward the long restful evening
and the croak of the night heron over the river at dark.

✄ THE OLD MAN CLIMBS A TREE

He had a tall cedar he wanted to cut for posts,
but it leaned backward toward the fence,
and there's no gain in tearing down one
fence to build another. To preserve the fence
already built, he needed to fasten a rope
high up in the cedar, and draw it tight
to the trunk of another tree, so that as he sawed
the cedar free of its stance it would sway
away from the fence as it fell. To bring
a ladder would require too long a carry
up through the woods. Besides, you can't
climb into a cedar tree by means of a ladder—
too bristly. He would need first to cut off
all the branches, and for that would need a ladder.

And so, he thought, he would need to climb
the tree itself. He'd climbed trees many times
in play when he was a boy, and many times
since, also, when he'd had a reason. He'd loved
always his reasons for climbing trees.
But he'd come now to the age of remembering,
and he remembered his boyhood fall from an apple tree,
and being brought in to his mother, his wits
dispersed, not knowing where he was,
though where he was was this world still.
If that should happen now, he thought,
the world he waked up in would not be this one.

The other world is nearer to him now.
But trailing his rope untied as yet to anything
except himself, he climbed up once again and stood
where only birds and the wind had been before,

and knew it was another world, after all,
that he had climbed up into. There are
no worlds but other worlds: the world
of the field mouse, the world of the hawk,
the world of the beetle, the world of the oak,
the worlds of the unborn, the dead, and all
the heavenly host, and he is alive
in those worlds while living in his own.
Known or unknown, every world exists
because the others do.

             The treetops
are another world, smelling of bark,
a stratum of freer air and larger views,
from which he saw the world he'd lived in
all day until now, its intimate geography changed
by his absence and by the height he saw it from.
The sky was a little larger, and all around
the aerial topography of treetops, green and gray,
the ground almost invisible beneath.
He perched there, ungravitied as a bird,
knotting his rope and looking about, worlded
in worlds on worlds, pleased, and unafraid.

There are no worlds but other worlds
and all the other worlds are here,
reached or almost reachable by the same
outstretching hand, as he, perched upon
his high branch, almost imagined flight.
And yet when he descended into this other
other world, he climbed down all the way.
He did not swing out from a lower limb
and drop, as once he would have done.

James Bertolino

❧ See Willow

At last you'll know why you came.
See willow. See willow.
Hold to the proof of loons.
This day is like no other.

See willow. See willow.
Feel the slender spirit of the reeds.
This day is like no other.
Step wisely among the stones.

Feel the slender spirit of the reeds.
There are crows discussing the moon.
Step wisely among the stones.
The towhee says believe.

There are crows discussing the moon.
Feel wind inside the cedar.
The towhee says believe.
A star descends and everything rises.

Feel wind inside the cedar.
Hold to the proof of loons.
A star descends and everything rises.
At last you'll know why you came.

᧔ SNAIL RIVER

Here is the proposition that heals
with a caress of eagle feather,

that pulls a mountain range
through the wing-bone of a wren
to let it blossom.

The endless forms of the one thing, sunflower
as cougar's eye, glacier, underwater spider
with its bubble of air, slow river of snail, spiral
nebula—the way everything moistens
with love, hastens with fire.

Everywhere mouths are opening and closing,
gills turning ocean to lace, baleen
counting the smallest lives. It's time for

computers to swoon
to the symphonic order of termite
cathedrals: bravo, bravo!

Dance of the gift of living crystal. The virtuous

ballets of erectile tissue, a sweetness
in the hydraulic whistling
of the black widow's musculature: such intelligence.

Listen to the shrill piping of silica
inside the high Douglas fir.
Hear everywhere the electron's bright chirp
and the deep hum of the Earth
saying "home."

Sallie Bingham

✑ SPRING HOUSE

Descend at your peril into the spring house.
You will find there Jewel Weed and briar,
the binding smell of urine tamped down
in closely-packed dirt.

The stone top of the spring house is vaulted.
Time and pain went into the laying
and the eye of a prophet or farmer,
raising unknowing the tomb-shape of Eqypt

that century still buried.
Wasps circle the filled-in rectangle
that once let a ray of light creep
over milk jugs placed by the streamlet

long ago dried up and forgotten.
Fall's with us again; a new road
slashes the woods by the spring house.
A crow cries imminent destruction.

Yet water outlasts every outcome,
and stones, tossed by the bulldozer, rest
under the mud and the rubble; nothing
erases the shape of the spring house,
though the arc of its vaulted roof fall,

though the last drop of moisture is taken.

Steven Blevins

ๆ NEW YORK

Birds even in the city
survive to sing about sun-
light straining through the gritty breath
of New York.

Tulips, perfect orange
and pink
wide-spread petals
stand miraculously
unpicked.

There are horses in blinders
tracing concrete circles
around Central Park,
energy throttled at the mouth,
broken.

The elephant caught in its cage
is a beast to see
and be reminded
of the animals who imprison
in order to admire.

Philip Booth

ᴄᵖ BEE

A bumbler for sure.
Got caught between the
window and screen. How
he got in, God only.
House as closed to
the world as I've
been all day, numb
to much I'm supposed
to love. But tried,
at least, to care
for the bumbler.

Took a glass tumbler,
a red Ace of Hearts:
slipped the glass over
the bee buzzing anger.
Then the card under,
to give myself cover.

Took the whole show
to the sideyard door:
at the sill, tipped
the tumbler then slipped
the card. Bee took off
into wavery life.

Didn't do much this
slow day in mid-spring.
Did one good thing:
helped an old bee go.

✤ WITHIN

A peninsula church, October's last Sunday.
Outside, a half-gale. Barely beyond the twelve-
over-twelve high panes of the Southwest window,

frost-paled maple leaves, still stemmed to
their half-stripped tree, stream a bright translucence.
Sunstruck, cloudstruck, horizon-bound by

the seawind, they outshine the sermon, the hymns,
the words of the congregation's oldest prayer.
Given the leaves' light, their benediction, matched

by the Bach *partita* fallen or risen to us through
its thousand seasons, we feel our lives bare: without
guilt or reason, we let our eyes fill and be lifted.

Robert Bringhurst

   ↶   FROM *Conversations with a Toad*

Behind you: the owl, whose eyes
have no corners: the owl with her quick
neck, who faces whatever she sees.
The raven, with voices like musselshell, wellwater, wood.
The dippers with voices like water on water.
The ruffed grouse drumming in the Douglas-fir.
And the heron flying in whole notes,
the kingfisher crossing in dotted eighths
and in quarters—both silent; much later,
two voices like washboards:
one bass, coarser than gravel,
one mezzo, crushed gravel and sand.

Their beauty bites into the truth.
One way to fail to be is to be merely
pretty. But that beauty: it feeds on you; we
feed on it. As you feed on this
moth, toad, or may: he may yet be
your dinner: his hazelnut tonsure,
the face like a goat's but clean,
and the mane like brown cornsilk.
Nerves spring from his forehead like fernfronds,
like feathers. He too is transformed.
This is the last life, toad.
Those who eat will be eaten. That
is the one resurrection.

We who kill not to eat but to mark
our domain—to build and breed, in place
of what is, what we choose to create—
have reduced by that much the population of heaven.

Under the sunrise the mountains
are walking on water.
This is the skin.
The mountains are dancing.
They are walking on their toes
on all the water in the world.
This is the blood.
And all the water in the world—
oceans, raindrops, runoff dipped
in cupped hands, moistened lips and tears—
is holding up the mountains.
This is the ligament. This is the bone.

The bones are flowing water.
There is marrow in the bone.
Never judge by just one world.
In the marrow is the blood.
If the mountains stop walking, the world
will stop being born.

Joseph Bruchac

☞ SPRING PEEPERS

Their voices are thin as lines of rain.
They pierce the night like tribal singers,
threading songs into the beat of the drum,
notes shrill and strong as cries of birth.

I hear them where the edge of the field
slopes down into brush and flowing darkness.
There the swamp fills the night with a presence
more complete than any memory's directions.

Rain falls sudden as seeds from a sower's hands.
It is what they chant for, the high-throated ones.
As they call to each other, they call for moisture,
the rain of new life, where embryo eyes
brighter than jewels surge in masses of eggs.

Finding my way home, I carry their song,
one hand shading my eyes against the cool rain
which soaks through my clothes, beads my brows with crystal,
each drop a note throbbing my skin, singing, singing,
singing.

Hayden Carruth

☞ THE SOFT TIME OF THE YEAR

At last, at last the night
    lies down beneath the hill
and the busy city in the sky
    becomes visible. What
a bustling and confusion of
    activity up there! I
can see the rape of Helen
    and hear my own first cry
when I was born, for both
    of which I feel profoundly
sorry. Somewhere nearby
    meanwhile a paleolithic
relentless whippoorwill
    confides his commentary.

Robin S. Chapman

❧ YOUR FACE HERE

All the laughing girls wait for the hands
Of the cameraman to position their heads
On the video screen, where he erases the face
Of a body-building beach girl in G-string
And inserts the posing person's head,
Suddenly stilled in its slant and laugh,
Atop the muscular neck—a mask; he clips
Pixels, smooths hairline, brushes wrinkles.
The thought arises of the codes we know
That can be cut and spliced almost as easily,
Creating the perfectly shaped, tough tomato,
The mute, immobile, meaty chicken,
As though, in some choose-your-future shop,
We could stand in line, picking the season's
Desirable eye shape, body, smile—and none
Of the laughing girls would be here at all.

Peter Cooley

ᛩ THE SECRET

Because I was too much with myself
and myself, I went down to the sea this evening.
The tide was in, and all along the sand
the dead were waiting: auger & whelk,
pectin & conch, cast up, cast back again,
rattling their spines, the green waves diced with foam.
The sea looked straight at me
it wouldn't flinch, this funny cemetery
while I stretched out among the tombs
surrendering the black light in my limbs,
my head, to drown it.

And now, sitting here tonight
I hear the dead at my desk
talking to the dead, lamenting.
The sea stalls in my arms & legs,
knocks at my eyes, asking for a word, any word.

I had no one to tell this to but you.

W. S. Di Piero

Why not violate sense and say
that inside bud or acorn there's
biological will, some decisive
push inside flowering, a wish
for divisive embodiment
giving form to every instant,
intentional beginnings that spiral
to bright emergence? It's like
the heartbeat in your belly
late at night, the baffled need
that gives a metric to your voice:
I checked the wateroak today
and realize it budded overnight,
first nothing but scraggly tips
then those bulging green points
shaped like flames stopped.

Sharon Dolin

☞ MY SOUL'S WARDROBE

> *By all means use sometimes to be alone;*
> *salute thyself; see what thy soul doth wear;*
> —George Herbert, "A Church Porch" xxv

Today I'll wear a cool summer coat
an anxious spray of blue-green needles
porcupine of the tall Scotch pine.

Later I'll wear a lake of slate-grey hope
shivery weather with lots of heather
loose foliage of late summer alpine.

By late morning I'll sport a scarf of wind at my throat
not too lazy, very hazy, impatient weather
of wanting to swim in this woodsy pond by wild lupine.

Or else by midday I'll doff a cap and row a boat
out to the shimmery island of black walnut trees
and wild blueberries where goldenrod wave in a line.

By afternoon I'll don my cape of white oak
and go find a pure oak stand where I'll sit
as still as a tree or a bird or a vine of spicy woodbine.

Michael Dorris

⃠ PREY

Crooked in the skyward angle of a pyramid
Your foreleg dangles from the tailgate,
The only motion as your body
Measures width above the license.

It joggles, so slender that even by fours
I marvel it balanced your weight
Like a Danish table, all points
Centered at some invisible heart.

And now it beckons superfluous, string
Without meat, a hoof souvenir
Ashtray for plaid gunners,
Orange-hatted, smoking in pairs.

Constance Egemo

∽ SILVER POPLAR AT SUNRISE

Poplar,
in this morning light
you come into another life.

The current of air
moves you to silver,
green-silver,
green.

You show me your earth-face,
you show me your spirit-face,
as though we were the same species.
As though we were lovers.

Richard Elman

ᵍ OCTOBER OBSERVED, HUDSON FALLS, NEW YORK
IN BILL'S BACK YARD

(for William Bronk)

The whole afternoon glistening
on a string bean pole. The beans
toughening to that light
are big hard grey
green beans,
dirty fingers reaching
toward this light.

Above the rotten melon heads,
half-gnawed tomatoes,
and cucumber scars,
a last spray of cornflowers
almost as pale as
this cold cloudless sky.

The cat's learning to fly—
to feed three baby birds
on the roof of
his mouth. The enormity
of their tiny separate
gaping needs
and his fiercely furred shadows.

Charles Fishman

✑ WHAPMAGOOSTUI

Hydro-Québec in James Bay Wilderness
November 1992

A silence wells up at the mouth
of the river, north of Québec,
in the haunted light of a culture . . .
silence deep as the bay, burden
of many rivers: Eastman and Moose,
Nottaway and Attawapiskat, the La Grande
and this, that rolls and flashes
beneath us, *Whapmagoostui*, the Great
Whale. Miles of dark-green black spruce
and white spruce, taller ash-barked, dress
and guardian hills. Here, millennia
of ponds have glittered in the first light,
translucent as blown glass or turbid, hue-
shifting, like molten pewter; lakes polished
smooth in the near-Arctic sun: trays of native
silver; rivers swollen with pike, whitefish, salmon;
geese in the rippled streams, snowy owls in the darkening
branches; caribou chesting the current, endless
tide of blood, meat, hide, horn, bone, music.

After sundown, a red hunter's moon rises
over the stalking grounds of the Cree nation.
Lodges are fragrant with elk skins, with evergreen
boughs. The night is bisected, then quartered,
by shimmering light that spangles the black dream
of hills. Water burns with the light.

For 5,000 years, the people sat around this fire:
chanted, gave thanks, grieved, laughed
and remembered. Ancestors are buried here.

A cry spirals up like the rasp of a red-tailed hawk.

Brendan Galvin

℘ BULLFROG

Maybe you escaped from the marsh
when that heron began scarfing
all it could into its gaping rictus,
lining blue skin and bones
against what was coming. You were
no stone ornament on those rocks
around the garden pool, slickskin,
rubberhead, and we loved your virid
look of a critic assessed for back taxes.
There were signs and portents enough:
in those days with yellow-rumped
warblers fugitive in their margins,
we brought in the fantails
and black mollies. Fieldmice began
shifting their bones and slipping
their envelopes of skin into the shed
behind your pool, strewing turds
delicate as lettuce seeds, balling up
nests in our Santa stuff. One night
in Ellen's sleep a Canada goose
swam in the pool, eating the water hyacinths
and bamboo. Told to scram, "Can we talk?"
it inquired, then climbed into
a lawnchair that collapsed with the dream.
What else to say about you? Aesop
would have known. Maybe something about
understanding when to make the leap?
On Twelfth Night you said nothing.
After the Snow Moon, owls brought their

courtship delirium around; ice on the pool
released you, eyes buttoned tight,
your tongue giving my sympathies
the year's first raspberry.

ↄ AN INSIDE JOB

We are in over your head.
Explain our night-moves
as a few leaves trying
for braille on a wall,
but I and my kind
are between you and the day,
inhabiting spaces you own
but have never seen.
Inquisitive to a fault,
though not acquisitive,
goblets, copper-bottomed pots,
pond ripples caught and held
in well-grained cabinetry,
all the appointments of your life
are our debris. Free
your house's waters, retract
its light, and when stars
over this rooftree drip
cold, our brainy hands remember
the way to the old denning place,
ours before you strained oceanic light
through such tall glass, and made
pasta by hand, before Algonquians
named us *arahkunem*. Night
stirs in branches, but in time
we're a smell you cut after
through our floor and we see you

down there. Our young huddle
in a corner, but a few of us pad over
and look in on you,
bystanders at a construction site.

❧ THE MAIL FROM RIGHT HERE

Her wings inferring
the sound of a Vespa
of forty years ago,
she is two feet away
in her sheath of implied
green, among red blossoms
of the emperor pole beans
like a lifetime's
remembered kisses, her
white tailband a brush
meekly dipped, and now
she is here, face
to my face, making me glad
the first time for
bifocals, this ounce
that leaves and arrives
when she will, turns
at the rate of
a flowerhead,
reverses herself
on the idea of a dime,
and a few feet into the air
is air.

Better to dream away this profound June dusk
on old loves or an ancient Chevrolet
than squander it on this Briggs and Stratton
choir, this davening with clippers
around the edges. Let go and let
daisy fleabane, deepen a little
and try to feel how much worse
the moles feel under those blades
than you when a chopper passes over the roof.
Cancel once and for all the pleading of
maimed hearts you hear beneath horsepower,
and the phone ringing in the kitchen
to say your ship's come in. Let these blues
turn bluets, violets, blue-eyed grass,
swing an occasional scythe without tripping
a grasshopper out of exhausted dew,
sneer at the man from Chlorophyll who primes
neighborhood grass into the happiness
of new toothpastes. Wait for November,
and the red fruiting clusters of Russian olives.
Then cedar waxwings will come, masked,
sleek, crested birds colored
like cars you used to think you'd own.

Kenneth Gangemi

✧ NOTES OF A MOONWATCHER

The moon never lets me down.
It is my good friend, constant
and reliable. Two nights after
new moon I look for the slim
crescent, low in the west at sunset.
Then begins the glorious waxing,
the better half of the lunar month.
The crescent is most beautiful
on the third night after new moon.
Shakespeare looked at the moon,
and Baudelaire, and Walt Whitman.
It is a brotherhood that spans
the centuries. Poets have written
about the crescent moon and
full moon, but never about the
gibbous moon, clearly a neglected
phase. More complex than a full
moon are the nights before, when
the earlier rise interacts with the
setting sun. Four nights before
full moon I once saw sunshine
on the western clouds and moonshine
on the eastern clouds. The sunset
in the west lowered and dimmed,
the moon in the east rose and
brightened. The full moon always
rises at sunset and is different
in every season. In summer it

is low and sensual, more observed
and enjoyed. In winter it is
high and brilliant. Tu Fu once
said, 'The same clear glory
extends for ten thousand miles.'

Faye George

ꝯ SHAGBARK

Not a pretty tree,
it is grandly shabby, inhabiting its name,
the long throat of itself spoken of earth.

Self-contained,
lone and tall at the edge of the wood,
trailing its ragged cloak

through the blue smoke of autumn;
shedding bark, leaf, a hard-shelled fruit
husked in pungent rind.

Magnificent in moonlight,
half tree, half animal,
rampant shadow of the wood.

Hair-shirt flagellant
when the wind comes
full of its own ragged breath,

the leaf stripper
ripping pages of October
twig from limb, thrown

to the mercy of the grass
with the hatched nut nested in its rind,
spanked green and blighted brown.

Burst crescents
staining the nail with tannin,
astringent, burnt-lime,

a taste that sings on the tongue.
And the sweet, chambered meat
at the nugget's heart.

∽ WILDERNESS

This place has no nakedness,
filling itself with the seasons.
The rocks arrange themselves for leisure.
The trees work at their own pace.
The ponds collect a depth.

We say the day is raw and cold.
The day dismisses us,
retreating into the reeds, the pines,
the frost-burnt mosses, the day
with its roots in winter now,
in the old, slow growth.

Lovely because it is empty.

Eamon Grennan

ꝏ SHORELINE AFTER STORM

Caught between catastrophe and habit
the heron stockstill at the tip of the inlet
where a hard dry crumble of mud sees
its first light in millennia. A midden of
periwinkle shells glitters in beige ground
where brief unrecorded lives have left us
only this sign of themselves, a poor page
from the history book of their hunger.
Two mink go floating over the rocks
like oil—one foxy coloured, the other
a melting shade of chocolate: survival
artists, they live off what's possible,
keeping house where they can. As this
squeaking tern does in its aerodynamic
lack of fuss, entering a wavecrest
where the streamlined stickleback is
one knowing muscle from teeth to tail,
its own history nothing but biology
as it leans into the shapemaking arms
of hunger and its abrupt, provisional
satisfactions. On your own two feet
that retreat from water, leave mud
behind, you're passing through, picked
by quick winds, a shadow travelling
the sprawled bodies of rocks made
light of by the storm's heavy matters
that have changed the face of things
again, between night and morning.

Aimée Grunberger

☞ THE OLD ROAD

The old road curves off the highway.
A few clapboard or brick houses remain,
nestled in a wide arc, grassed-in.
Pavement Ends, the sign might read.

The old road climbs for awhile,
then an equal and opposite curve
rejoins it to the passing stream.
We need it more than it needs us.

The old road once fed all these towns
along the Eastern coast. Piece by piece,
material traces reconstruct it: two parallel
ruts in the frozen mud, a broken line

charted by the Geological Survey,
an alleé between the stoutest trees,
two specimen oaks standing sentry
at an empty cellar hole.

May roadside archaeologists
endlessly rediscover these remnants
of our pedestrian past,
too well-trammeled to call history.

∿ SWIMMING UPSTREAM

This frog is more gifted
than mere appearance would indicate.
Like a finely-tuned bard, like the prince's courtesan,
your tongue is the right hand of desire.

And speaking of hands, they are all but useless.
Do not attempt to grasp what you cannot have.
Allow your powerful legs and batwing feet
to launch you across the dragging current.

And, for God's sake and your own, leap!
From dry land to outcropped boulder,
at spring torrent or seven-year drought,
the gift of air and motion can be yours.

From birth, you are one thing,
then you become yourself forever.
Fishtail recedes as backbone curves and ossifies.
Your hide turns green and stubborn.

Those bulbous eyes can split the water,
rake the shore, while you, the beast, remain
camouflaged in tall grass, baking off pond muck,
blissed-out on a rock in the April sun.

Mud is second skin, water and earth your twin allies,
so when night carves its initial on the river's path,
still those leaping feet, that whipping tongue.
Lift up your gullet for passing low notes and wail.

John Haines

ECLIPSE

You will speak of our days in whispers
if the twilight wins.

How from our camp on the hill
we saw below us the river whiten,
the town lamps flicker and sink,
and all the traffic muted.

A little wind in the ice-bound grass,
the clouds parting—
half-shielded in the overcast,
a round face swallowed the sun.

No one came near to tell us
why our shadows faded from the snow,
nor why in that sudden dusk
the chilled flocks, black and strange,
rose up about us—then
settled in the field without a sound.

As once in another country,
at the height of noon,
the summer birds stopped singing
and night came back . . .

So now as then might the year
be ending before the soil was broken,
and summer itself become
a cold sleep inside the sun.

᧐ ROADSIDE WEEDS

From Asia, the stony Rift,
from the rank thicket
we have come,
water-borne and wind-carried.

I was once a seed
swollen in a birdcrop,
and you like a tick
traveled in a bale of wool.

We are pest and bounty,
we possess the yard
and claim the field.

Here stands an immigrant
with his heel in the dust,
alien as Black Medick:
Great Mullein,
lord of the roadside.

Whatever is here is native,
never to be erased
from the chosen ground.

Our roots drink that water,
from the burst pod
a welcoming wind scatters
our seed,

in that field, or this one.

ᴄᶠ YETI

I

Our years are driven wild,
and the fear-changed mind
of the people turns once again
to its brute solace—
the night-coursing of monsters,
emblems of blood,
in the sleep of reason.

How often has the stalled
mountaineer awakened,
to hear far down the moonlit
col, the snow-filled cry
of a beast that mates
once in a hundred years.

Out of its cage of sleep
a maimed and shaggy captive
climbs shelf by shelf
and ridge by ridge to a cave
warmed in the icefields,
stuck with hair
and stained with blood.

II

In this world we think we know,
something will always
be hidden, whether a fern-rib
traced in the oldest rock,

or a force behind our face,
like the pulse of a reptile,
dim and electric.

John Haines   55

A possibility we hadn't
thought of, too tall
and thick to be believed.

Its face like a wise ape
driven to the snows,
turns at the starry ford,
gives back one burning
look, and goes.

Brian Henry

✐ MORAINE LAKE

I read my face on smooth stones.
Glacial silt lacquers water milky green.
Mountains rise then plunge into glass.
Clouds float, subaqueous.

I read mountains in glass:
Glacial silt rises, subaqueous.
Mountains float, milky green.
Clouds lacquer smooth stones.

I read water, milky green.
Glacial silt floats in glass.
Mountains lacquered, subaqueous
Clouds rise then plunge in water.

William Heyen

❧ CRANE IN REEDS

Ants ate half its left wing.
Its right eye socket filled with marsh mud,
its left with bluish maggots.
Glistening close around it, razor reeds
almost always swayed.

Gibbs Pond gave me the dead crane.
I was nine, the only one
to see it, day by day, all summer,
molt down, rot, feed flies, disappear except
for beak, skeleton, a few feathers.

Now, in what seems to be a dream
but no one knows, I kneel beside that boy
beside the crane. We are only
a little afraid as we stare at the vivid
dead thing again. Glory

is clearly with it despite
reed stillness
and maggots bluing down to bone.

ᴏᴄ DERAILMENT

A quarter-million, the last great flock of passenger pigeons,
nested in April, 1896, near Bowling Green, Ohio.

By telegraph, word spread. By horse & rail, shooters
& trappers arrived. 200,000 bodies were kept;

40,000 mutilated & wasted; countless newborn chicks
not yet at the fattened squab stage, & thus worthless,

destroyed; maybe 5,000 birds escaped this harvest
(one of which might have been "Martha,"

dies 1 September 1914 in Cincinnati,
29 years old, the last of her species, but, no,

she was born in captivity, but maybe her mother,
but, no, this doesn't compute either) . . . .

In any case,

to help preserve their breast meat
the pigeons' crops were cut out,

the edible kill of this occasion shipped toward
markets in the east, but derailment occurred . . . .

Under an unseasonably hot spring sun,
the dead birds packed in boxes began to putrefy

& all 200,000 carcasses were dumped
into a deep ravine a few miles from the depot . . . .

ᴄ⸱ EMANCIPATION PROCLAMATION

Whereas it minds its own business
& lives in its one place so faithfully
& its trunk supports us when we lean against it
& its branches remind us of how we think

Whereas it keeps no bank account but hoards carbon
& does not discriminate between starlings and robins
& provides free housing for insects & squirrels
& lifts heartwood grave into the air

Whereas it holds our firmament in place
& writes underground gospel with its roots
& whispers us oxygen with its leaves
& suffers stress in its new climate of ultraviolet

We the people for ourselves & our children
necessarily proclaim this tree
free from commerce & belonging to itself
as long as it & we shall live.

☞ WINDFALL

Eating an apple, I think of Emerson
in another railroad berth
traveling to another Chautauqua. This time,

maybe it's summer, he's passing
apple orchards in Ohio where
he half dreams a bumblebee

sipping nectar—in its belly, a mite
glows with mite joy. In the mite's belly,
other living things the size of atoms

climb mountains, . . . but he's tired
of revelation. It's certain the cosmos
is an orchard, or tree, or single bee

bearing the whole apple future, & Boston,
from one field to another,
& bearing him. He'll lecture this audience

to find & live the secret of any windfall,
to try, for god's sake, to love
that which is obvious, & themselves.

Patricia Hooper

∽ AUGUST

A chipmunk has made its nest
under the porch, and the bees
thrive in the loose mortar, filling
the walls of my house

with honey. I've come out
barefoot in damp grass
and gathered my own store
of baby's breath and a bright

harvest of everlastings.
The phlox opens. The scent
of cider already ripens
in the apple tree, and whatever

bitterness sent me plunging
into the yard has flown
to another body, less
distracted by circumstance.

Ben Howard

Mute as it is, the river
fashions its signature.

Its waves are not the waves
of sorrow or remorse

nor its toll the toll of anger.
Here are its foul banks,

its waters slapping hulls,
its levees strewn with rubble.

Here is its dreaded rising,
its savage intransigence,

spilling across the quarrels
of faction, race, and gender—

as though its spoiled waters,
surging through streets and houses,

could void the heart of malice
or rectify disorder.

↝ THE RIVER'S ANSWER

In me they dump their cans, their toilet paper,
Their broken fishing-lines. I teem with their
Debris. I am the one who swallows whole
And gurgitates their rubbish, part and parcel.
What do they know of my intelligence,
My way of cleansing what they cast aside?
In me a gullet greater than their own
Takes in the common folly of the world
And makes of insolence its daily bread.
What do they know of my resilience,
Which eats the shell but leaves the soul intact?
Replete with memory and fortitude,
My fluent heart takes refuge in the fact
That I will be extant when they are gone.

Coral Hull

The moon moves up the outback ridge & they turn chewing,
Raised on haunches to test & taste the night,
One ripple in the long grass or an owl dropping,
& the whole mob is spooked into flight,
Old boomers & blue flyers, from rocky ranges to open plains,
Remote & fabulous creatures, that spring into life,
Across the land where the sun has crossed the wind,
Following the heat that rises through the ground,
With tales of further ahead or far behind,
& eyes to cover the distance from left to right,
The history of the old macropods,
Told through the length & height of leaps,
& airborne bulk, over tangles of fence & crooked gates,
& haunted grey crossings of dry creek beds,
A tail lever forcing take-off, a rudder for varying hops & turns,
To the drinking places & to the sides of roads,
For shots of water sweetened with grass shoots,
Or midday wary beneath shady blue gums, or on the move at dusk,
Or edgy at night, in the sub divided paddocks,
& brackish white above the whisker mark,
As the tide of dawn rises up their faces, until the blood is warm,
& they are lit, into the action of flying,
Yet the land that flew fades so quickly,
In a pile of skins, exposed to sunlight, in a shooters' camp.

David Ignatow

✑ SUBURBIA

The silence of the suburb
its woods primeval dark.
Cars drive through,
their lights
timidly centered
straight down the road

Mark Irwin

☞ GIVE

Floating along the tops of the Sangre de Christos
the slow popcorn of clouds.
All day the summer wears us like an invisible gown
and the wind whispers *It is the outside*
you can never have, whispers this through the trees,
their great breathing lungs. Rivers flood.
The creek smells like a root

split open. Enter those
with nothing. Come in. At midnight
we flooded the field, stood in the oozing muck to dream
the hayfield brightening like fire. River me
with desire,—here, here, and here

we wade through stars, flesh to their
skeletal design. In the pitch black a calf
bawls. To give is the future
tense of to have.

✑ A TREE

There was the tree the day they planted
it, a celebration of all he desired to grow, stubborn
at first, then mapling out over the yard for birthdays,
weddings, its leaves always adding, counting
something difficult to see, like a lake
glimpsed through the trees. They

married, the leaves thickened, summer
building its anniversary, a deep green air whispering
children, —a boy, girl, —spring
following spring, the budding, rivering leaves never
quite still, watching, stirring the air they

breathed.—Whose memory they
were? Autumn colored it pear-yellow, a nearer
sun. He raked with his wife, while Kit and Tina
ran and fell head first in the paper
fruit of the leaves. Branches, tuff-boned, emptying, veined

against blue, etched out its being, its drowsy
will. Winters gave it a whirring
music, a hushed violining: the crown bunting snow. Ghostly
the tree anchored, white becoming islanded
green. Winters to springs, and summers'

reservoir still, then ten sleeps in which bikes leaned, lawn mowers
whirred, kids grew, kissed, left home
and married, the great crown of leaves now
a lake of green whispering, memory
is a paradise extending what will not

expel. Leaves, spatulate, thickened, and the tented
shade grew, a memory grows, illumined, storied
with desire, dusk-lit, haloed green dissolving
toward blue. And that far winter, as he was dying
he drew the ones he loved in pencil, and asked
them to color it in, after he was gone.

George Keithley

၅ FIRST MORNING

Autumn is finished—yesterday a flash
storm, the worst since my father's death,
then last night's freeze. At once granite
outcrop wears a milky glaze; all
the lean hemlocks are sheathed in ice.
At dawn walking from the meadow
to the woods I wish for the warmth
of his voice. A peaceable man—only
injustice angered him. How might
we meet again if not hiking
in these frosted fields? No hunter,
he loved to discover animals
in their habitat then leave them
undisturbed. Which he thought just.
"They earn their peace among us.
Let them be." The wren in its nest;
the half-dozen frogs surviving
—who can say how—in a bog-hole;
two owls attracted to the gloom
of the horse barn.

                    His patience will take
years to learn—it's time I start home
to my own children. Emerging
from a stand of pines shagged with cold,
the needles silvered overnight,
I surprise a fox and it bolts
to safety. Bushy tail barely
twitching the ghostly grass or ice-
crusted manzanita, it leaves

little trace. Shafts of sunlight strike
an opaque blue-white sheen which clings
to the country road. It's the first
morning of winter and the world
is made of glass the heart must break.

Maurice Kenny

∽ WILD FLOWER

The throat
of a peanut butter jar
clutches a fistful
of black-eyed susans
erect before the glass-
window magnifying
the high wooded hill
behind. One blossom
stretches on a single leg
reaching for the sun
as it darkens; birch silvers—
foil caught in a last ray.
Such simplicity must
not go un-noticed.

Ursula K. Le Guin

✒ RIDING ON THE "COAST STARLIGHT"

I saw white pelicans rise
from the waters of morning
in the wide valley, going.
I saw trees white with snow
rise silent from clouds
in the deep mountains, returning.
Heavy, noble, solemn the gesture
of the wings, the branches,
a white writing on destruction.

Denise Levertov

∽ PROTESTING AT THE NUCLEAR TEST SITE

A year before, this desert
had raised its claws to me,
importunate and indifferent, half-naked beggar
displaying sores at the city gates.
Now again, in the raw glare
of Lent. Spikes, thorns, spines.
Where was the beauty others perceived?
I could not.
                    But when the Shoshone elder spoke,
last year and now once more,
slowly I began to see what I saw as ugly were marks
of torture. When he was young this was desert, too,
but of different aspect, austere but joyful.
A people's reverence illumined stony ground.
Now, as my mind knew but imagination failed to acknowledge,
deep, deep and narrow the holes were bored
into the land's innards, and there, in savage routine,
Hiroshima blasts exploded, exploded, rape
repeated month after month for years.
What repelled me here was no common aridity
unappealing to lovers of lakes and trees,
but anguish, lineaments drab with anguish. This terrain
turned to the human world a gaze
of scorn, victim to tormentor.
                              Slowly,
revulsion unstiffened itself, I learned
almost to love
the dry and hostile earth, its dusty growth
of low harsh plants, sparse in unceasing wind;
could almost have bent
to kiss that leper face.

Composed by nature, time, human art,
an earthly paradise. A haze that is not smog
gentles the light. Mountains delicately frosted,
timbered autumnal hillsides copper and bronze.
Black-green of pine, gray-green of olive.
Nothing is missing. Ferries' long wakes pattern the water,
send to the still shores a minor music of waves.
Dark perpendiculars
of cypress, grouped or single, cross immemorial
horizontals of terraced slopes, the outstretched wings,
creamy yellow, of villas more elegant
in slight disrepair than anything spick and span
could ever be. And all perceived
not through our own crude gaze alone but by the accretion
of others' vision—language, paint, memory transmitted.
Here, just now, the malady
we know the earth endures seems in remission—
or we are, from that knowledge that gnaws at us.
But only seems. Down by the lake the sign:
"Swim at your own risk. The lake is polluted."
Not badly, someone says, blithely irrelevant.
We can avoid looking that way,
if we choose. That's at our own risk.
Deep underneath remission's fragile peace,
the misshaped cells remain.

♔ A WREN

Quiet among the leaves, a wren,
fearless as if I were invisible
or moved with a silence like its own.

From bush to bush
it flies without hesitation,
no flutter or whirring of wings.
I feel myself lifted,
lightened, dispersed:

it has turned me to air,
it can fly right through me.

William Matthews

☞ NAMES

Ten kinds of wolf are gone and twelve of rat
and not a single insect species.
Three sorts of skink are history and two
of minnow, two of pupfish, ten of owl.
Seventeen kinds of rail are out of here
and five of finch. It comforts us to think
the dinosaurs bought their farms all at once,
but they died at a rate of one species
per thousand years. Life in a faster lane
erased the speckled dace, the thicktail chub,
two kinds of thrush and six of wren, the heath
hen and Ash Meadows killfish. There are four
kinds of sucker not born any minute
anymore. The Christmas Island musk shrew
is defunct. Some places molt and peel so fast
it's a wonder they have any name:
the Chatham Island bellbird flew the coop
as did the Chatham Island fernbird, the
Lord Howe Island fantail and the Lord Howe
Island blackbird. The Utah Lake sculpin,
Arizona jaguar and Puerto
Rican caviomorph, the Vegas Valley
leopard frog and New Caledonian lorikeet?
They've hit the road for which there is no name
a mouth surrounds so well as it did theirs.
The sea mink's crossed the bar and the great auk's
ground time here was brief. Four forms the macaw
took are cancelled checks. Sad Adam fills his lungs
with haunted air, and so does angry Eve:

they meant no name they made up for farewell.
They were just a couple starting out,
a place they could afford, a few laughs,
no champagne but a bottle of rose.
In fact Adam and Eve are not their names.

James C. McCullagh

❦ MERMAID'S SONG

She rose from the water like a mermaid.
Her hands were hearts, palms of water,
Fists of sand from the ocean floor.
Feet anchored in seaweed
She was the tide on my golden path,
Gave to me crystals,
Mirrors of sky, blue courage
And said: "The seas run south.
Join them. Rage like the clouds,
Cover your face with Jasmine and oil,
Leave your hair on land, your hearing
To the poor who wait patiently on corners,
Give your eyes to the first rose
So it may see the garden in a well of perfume,
Take your soul underwater, drift with the dolphins
Past Catalina, La Jolla, down the Baja,
Swim with the whales, hear the bird song
Move the marsh grass like an orchestra
Where the violins are thyme, the cellos basil,
Be the blue sea inside the green belly,
Push away the oak beam offered in charity.
When you are as cold and white as cod
Grow your hair again thick with ocean trees,
Arm yourself with fins and teeth and scales.
Rise in your fullness to light: At the meridian
You are wild, blessed, and free."

Carrington McDuffie

ꝯ FINALLY THE RAIN

Hearing the rain at last, I stepped out and saw the dark day
and the rain falling in the bushes and trees, sealing
the ivy-enclosed yard, and I saw
how the thick cluster of white blossoms
trembled on the end of their
heavily laden stem,
gathering raindrops into their fragrant crevices and overflowing,
and beyond the yard stretched a green field
blurred by rain
and the music that had filled my head when I was inside
faded and disappeared
as I stood under the dripping leaves
and watched the rain fall into the still and open-armed day.

Roger Mitchell

ᷓ IT

Everyone seems to be waiting for it
to happen. Though nobody quite knows what
it will be. Someone to fall down, perhaps,
the market's ultimate collapse, the end
of baseball. Gambling is on the increase.
People are suddenly dead or confused.
What could it mean if the grass refuses
to grow, the factory moves to the moon
or to Mexico? Who says we have to be
happy or part of the reason why? What is
the matter with Mary Jane, really?
Is it a case of simple rice pudding?
I'd like to talk sometime, but not now,
about certain deserted beaches.
The old kind, not this one. Who are
these men in moon suits, anyway,
and what are they doing with those long,
crab-like mechanical tweezers?
I mean sharks I can take, but blue sand?

⌒ NORTH

I had been watching them drift up and down
the channel for an hour, trying to see
against gray cloud and failing light what sort
of thing it was that looked like confetti,
blowing trash above a landfill, snow.
They drove upstream, beating in slow
somnolent strokes, then came back, beating
in the same persistent way. I listened.
It may have been the wind, but I don't remember
their cries. Though they must have cried.
      To themselves, at least.
One of them banked steeply and dropped a wing
into the water, just the tip. Another, the same.
They were here, certainly, but not for long.
You could see it the way they came down at last,
in twos and threes, packing together tightly,
stepping, it seemed, almost reluctantly
into the water. They did this three times,
      each time
exploding upward into vague barrelling
formations, then falling slowly to the water,
and always aimed, all of them, the same way.
North, as I now realize.
          The last time,
when the rolling swirl seemed to move upward,
when it was sky they wanted, and more sky,
I had to squint to keep from losing them.
The clouds kept shoving to the east, layer
on smudged layer, dragging the light with it.
At last I could see them only through glass

and only when they banked their darker gray
against the one that crept crazily
along the shore, the rocks, the trees fallen
face first into the water, and the water.
And then, as if on a blind cue, the swirl
collapsed, and a wedge, almost a wing,
assembled itself from the scattered flecks.

I'm not sure what happened next, after the thing
swung slowly around, headed the wrong way.
By then I knew that everything I'd seen,
even the drifting up and down, was part
of one thing, undertow and tide and the
                    dragging sand.
They turned, of course. It was mid May.
It was the way they turned, the way things turn
that are difficult. Ungraceful, slow,
appearing to lose purpose and direction,
liable to reversion, tentative.
But go, finally, the way they were always
meant to, though they were kept from knowing
what it would be. Or, like some I know,
knew it and refused.

Dear D., I'm in a place where history
can't reach, they say. I'm out here on the plain
where corn, chemically assisted, fills
a hog so full it staggers to its trough.
Where chickens lay in unison and sign
the song American. Where "family"

is a metaphor and "home" a way to sell.
The cows out on Moore's Pike moo like boosters
for the new shopping mall extension.
A woods the size of Florida's in flames,
and breeding's rocket blows apart. Who knows,
the world may come to Bloomington in time.

Already, condos claw up every hill
in sight. The refugees arrive. The world's
in flight, D., grabbing what it can
before it's gone.
It's gone, of course. The grabbing's just a game.
A hundred million on a side, no time-outs.

Gary Paul Nabhan

℘ Coming Out on Solid Ground After the Ice Age

Now we hear the tamarack fall
while gusts whip frozen dust up in the break.
In front of us, where icy water trickles from the glacier,
our gaze spreads coldly over all the rubble
and tries to colonize the barrens of our state.

Our state? A place extending well beyond
the frozen northlands, Bering Straits, terrain
which curls below the great depressions
to junk out stone, cinder and mud
in a terminal sort of ground.

Our state cares less about the last few thousand years
which wore its mountains down, carved its valleys,
and more about the growth beginning
down along the lumpy riverbeds flyways follow
expressways of ridges where bull elks bugle.

Statehood in its purest form
is a thin green cover developing in swales
a woodchuck which ascends and scents its territory
a muskrat or man who knows where he is
by the taste of the soil or chew of a cattail root.

Duane Niatum

The painter descends into the world
like the morning sun
on madrona branch, azalea and peony,
follows the gold thread passing stem,
leaf, petal, moss, mushroom and trunk,
twig and stone. With beetle
down to roots, he squats in the center
of the morning colors, adds
a stroke to the feelings circulating
like seeds, the myth loops of worms.

He stops before the slug's footpath,
his brush crawls over the pungent
earth into greener, finer weaves,
the dreams of the awakened soil.
Like a sun rattle he shakes with joy,
renders the figures in the garden
wildly pushing and pulling with abandon.
He moves deeper into their ballet,
back to bulb and grub, spider and fern.

☞ Rufous Hummingbird

You almost trip as you hear
it dart past the azalea shrubs
to the solitary fox-glove.
It wears the colors of the sky
while the season snatches another wing.

Immersed in the greenbean's
swift phrase, it also has a bill
for honeysuckle and apple.
Such plucky, sparse flights of this
green and red-throated spool

of dashing light, sets you in a body
so small and nimble you could walk
in a space where nerves dance on an earth
clover-patched and leaf-stalked.
Even rock-fence lichen float down this stream.

∽ The Salmon

Mother of salt and slate,
foam and storm, eye of crimson columbine;
sea flower carried by our shadow people
in a canoe on a horizon of mud and slime,
under the forest floor;

mixer of scale, bone, and blood,
nose of Thunderbird who answered her wave
as it passed our rainbow mountain;
mother of calm and deliverance,
the tongue's drum from the cliff.

High above the raven valleys
near the sea, dream fox
with the thread of the current in its mouth
touches the Elwha river twice
as she nestles her eggs in the gravel.
The roots of the wind's hair
build the birth cradle out of moon and tide.

Salmon Woman, a streaky
thrust at fertility, edges like Dawn-maker
up the slope, the thinning trail of the river.
Fever rattle of joy and tenacity,
gills bellow fullness and emptiness:
the songs of grandmothers
around Hadlock village fires that wove
our daughter into blankets and water dreamers.

Memory hasn't a chord of what the family lost.
For centuries village ancestors potlatched salmon's return
so we could dance on the water like bugs.

Today the stones quit asking not to betray
their ceremonies, our ears deaf to their winter
story of mountain, river, cormorant, red-flowering

currant. Our car tracks trample their children
who vanish down the street like moonlight
into gutters, our abbreviated hours.

Topaz stones brought us dream circles in order
to never forget where the earth's heart cracked.
Our shadows became ant fodder; we laughed

like flies and drank the blood from mirrors.
Flint raised his arm to the hummingbird's
fragrances, healing our eyes, spiky as sea urchins.

We ground Flint to a machine that exploded
with roadkill floating in toxins.
From a cave, ancestor stones gave us the cells

of trout, madrona, butterfly, eagle and grizzly,
gave us our birth song born of the sea,
gave us eagle feathers for the sunrise dance.

We chose instead to shoot the spotted-owl
from its borderless clarity,
turn off life like a video, including ours.

John O'Brien

REVELATION ON A SUMMER WALK

Out of the farmhouse,
and once through the yard
you leave the lower pasture
to the mute Angus cattle
somehow fused to their own blue shadows.
Past the shed, past the barn,
pausing only at the cemetery,
you begin to climb the slope.
Now through the scented pines
and on and further up
till at last, breathing hard,
you enter an unknown meadow.
Here the grass is lush
and long and fire green and
toward the meadow's center,
like some great branch of lightning
that has split the world,
stands a gigantic chestnut snag
so gray and stark, it seems
the only thing of three dimensions
in this painting called, "A Summer Day."
You walk to it as if compelled,
stand near enough to smell,
sunlight and sweet decay.
Look up now, tilt back your head.
The tree's stillness
is so perfect, so absolute,
the summer sky seems
a web of spinning blue.
Given voice, the tree would whisper,
"You are here."

Mary Oliver

∽ AT THE SHORE

This morning
   wind that light-limbed dancer was all
      over the sky while
         ocean slapped up against
            the shore's black-beaked rocks
row after row of waves
   humped and fringed and exactly
different from each other and
   above them one white gull
      whirled slant and fast then
         dipped its wings turned
            in a soft and descending decision its
leafy feet touched
   pale water just beyond
breakage of waves it settled
   shook itself opened
      its spoony beak cranked
         like a pump. Listen!
            Here is the white and silky trumpet of nothing.
Here is the beautiful Nothing, body of happy,
   meaningless fire, wildfire, shaking the heart.

↩ DESIGN

Something
in the night
ran up the hill,
heavy-limbed and with the knot

of its heart pounding
and made it,
spurting forward
under the plunging

spiked feet
of the owl,
who has left
his design

in the sand:
a trail of stars,
angry and
powerful.

Imagine it—
death
floating by,
turning

on his silent shoulder,
and falling.
The beautiful
golden eyes.

Imagine
whatever it was that ran,
like a huddle of silk,
into the mossy bog.

How the one rises
every night
out of the black pines
of starvation.

How the other
night after night
leaps
over the hill of sorrow.

Beautiful from his tail-tip,
which is white and nervous,
to his nose,
which is black and nervous.
And beautiful all in-between.
Beautiful, all his muscle and readiness.
Beautiful his cruel and snapping eyes.
Beautiful his craftiness.
Beautiful when he caught the rabbit
under the snowy lash of the moon.
Beautiful his lean body curled down to sleep one morning
at the edge of the pond,
beautiful the long lie of his patience,
beautiful his pounce.
Beautiful when he snapped the mouse
from the curly weeds.
Beautiful the flounce of his teeth plucking the gosling
from the cattails.
Beautiful his rough tongue breaking it open
under the half-feathered wing.
Beautiful his red neck lashing, his black claws gripping.
Beautiful his shoulders plunging into the underbrush.
Beautiful his soft belly sucked in, as he floated across the field.
Beautiful the flick of his tail.
Beautiful his burning body under the furnace of the sun.
Beautiful the motor of his dark heart in the dark wind.

Nothing, I thought, could come out of such small
and beautiful containers,
like beach pebbles,
a modest calligraphy
on a blue-green background.
That's why I know it's magic, because I saw them just like that
in the lark's nest,
when the lark herself, trotting like an old lady,
tried to lead me away
through the tall, blonde weeds,

and after looking inside that delicate palace,
and seeing how impossible it all was,

I did what she wanted

But I came back.
That's why I know there are three new larks in the world
a little larger than pebbles,
three mouths like three scraps of red flannel,
pendulous bellies,

and the lark herself, again, without a telling flutter,
walking on her stiff legs through the weeds

the tracks of the hungry fox, the rakings of high tide,
flung boards,
the little silver purses of sun-bleached mussels.

❧ POEM 12 FROM "WEST WIND"

The cricket did not actually seek the hearth,
but the thicket of carpet beneath the refrigerator.
The whirring above was company, and from it issued
night and day the most prized gift of the gods:
warmth. Especially in the evenings the cricket
was happy, and sang. Later, in the night, it
crept out. There was not a single night when it
did not find, sooner or later, a sweet crumb, and
a small plump seed of some sort between the floor
boards. Thus, it got used to hope. It revised
altogether its idea of what the world was like,
and of what was going to happen next, or, even,
eventually. It thought: how sufficient are these
empty rooms! It thought: here I am still, in my
black suit, warm and content—and drew a little music
from its dark thighs. As though the twilight
underneath the refrigerator were the world. As
though the winter would never come.

✒ RICE

It grew in the black mud.
It grew under the tiger's orange paws.
Its stems thinner than candles, and as straight.
Its leaves like the feathers of egrets, but green.
The grains cresting, wanting to burst.
Oh, blood of the tiger.
I don't want you just to sit down at the table.
I don't want you just to eat, and be content.
I want you to walk out into the fields
where the water is shining, and the rice has risen.
I want you to stand there, far from the white tablecloth.
I want you to fill your hands with the mud, like a blessing.

↶ SNAPSHOTS

Six black ibis
step through the black and mossy panels
of summer water.

Six times
I sigh with delight.

Keep looking.

The way a muskrat
in the snick of its teeth can carry
long branches of leaves.

Small hawks
cleaning their beaks
in the sun.

If you think daylight is just daylight
then it is just daylight.

Believe me these are not just words talking.
This is my life, thinking of the darkness to follow.

Keep looking.

The fox: his barking, in god's darkness, as of a little dog.
The flounce of his teeth.

Every morning
all those pink and green doors
into the sea.

↝ WAKING ON A SUMMER MORNING

Water
skidding down platforms of stone
ten miles
nothing to talk to but ferns

in the deep water
the eye of a trout
under a shelf of stone
not moving

no one will ever sully the water
the ferns will go on sleeping and dreaming
no one will ever find the trout
for a thousand years he will lie there, gleaming.

⌒ WINGS

My dog came through the pinewoods dragging a dead fox—
ribs and a spine, and a tail with the fur still on it.
Where did you find this? I said to her, and she showed
me. And there was the skull, there were the leg bones
and the shoulder blades.

I took them home. I scrubbed them and put them on a
shelf to look at—the pelvis, and the milky helmet.
Sometimes, in the pines, in the starlight, an owl hunches
in the dense needles, and coughs up his pellet—the vole
or the mouse recently eaten. The pellets fall through
the branches, through the hair of the grass. Dark flowers
of fur, with a salt of bones and teeth, melting away.

In Washington, inside the building of glass and stone, and
down the long aisles, and deep inside the wide drawers,
are the bones of women and children, the bones of old
warriors. Whole skeletons, parts of skeletons. They can't
get up. They can't fall. As white as pieces of the moon—
mute, catalogued—they lie in the drawers.

So it didn't take long. I could see how it was, and where
I was headed. I took what was left of the fox back to the
pinewoods and buried it. I don't even remember where.
I do remember, though, how I felt. If I had wings I would
have opened them. I would have risen from the ground.

Simon J. Ortiz

↶ LOOK TO THE MOUNTAIN

The following is a song. Here, sing it. You will know what I mean.

Always, it shall be this way.
Always, it shall be this way.
Always, it shall be this way.
Always, it shall be this way.

Tee-dyameeh.
Buu-nameeh.
Koo-wahmeeh.
Haa-nahmeeh.

To the North.
To the West.
To the South.
To the East.

Tee-dyameeh,
aishtuh Quutih guh-chahnih.
Buu-nameeh,
aishtuh Quutih guh-chahnih.
Koo-wahmeeh,
aishtuh Quutih guh-chahnih.
Haa-nahmeeh,
aishtuh Quutih guh-chahnih.

To the North,
a Mountain is standing.
To the West,
a Mountain is standing.
To the South,
a Mountain is standing.

To the East,
a Mountain is standing.

All around, in all the sacred directions of the Earth,
a Mountain is standing. Look!
And look from all the sacred directions of the Earth,
we are standing here!

Look to the Mountain.
Look from the Mountain.
Look all around and within.
Look within and all around.

In thankfulness, we see the Mountain.
In thankfulness, we see from the Mountain.
In thankfulness, we are standing with the Mountain.
In thankfulness, we are standing with each other.
Look to the Mountain, we are standing with the Mountain.
Look from the Mountain, we are standing with each other.

Always, it shall be this way.
Always, it shall be this way.
Always, it shall be this way.
Always, it shall be this way.

Do you see what I mean when you sing it?

John Peck

☞ MOUNT BROMLEY HYMN

Beekeepers' boxes
staggered
in colors up a hillside,
Mahler's hot waxes

through horns, muted brass,
ponds
planing pale at evening
through hanging grasses—

one chord, one wide chord
for the harp
waiting hugely in things,
tilting forward

for that one touch,
perhaps with the
period of a brash comet,
one loving touch.

ꝯ Woods Burial

At the rapids father and boy pitch in a young birch
   laid out by winter.

It is the March of mud roads and triggered hearts.
   That boy leaps as the limber corpse
   hurtles a chute, his father chuckles.

If they really knew what history is,
even though they're in it up to their necks,
they'd feel it, the tug, the cold tilt. They'd stand, shiver.

But how much smarter is that? And how am I better?
   It is that log I've got to be,
      shot straight, unstuck from the banks,
sluicing my woodlice through the white gates,
      hurling home.

Jim Peterson

✌ STAND STILL

I have walked here before
entered a chain link gate
at the end of a narrow dirt road
happy to see the weeds overtaking it
but knowing it is owned
somewhere circled on a map
I have arrived too late
to return home before dark
I have gathered the seeds
in my cuffs and socks and laces
undergone the inspections of owls and deer
as mindless in the moment of watching
as trees
I have entered the mask of the web
tiny builder diving for weeds
have heard the voices come back slowly
to meet my silence
and have tracked the crackling of leaves
over the whole long face of a hill

but never have I seen this place
in the light of so much moon and stars
leaves and needles shining on the ground
and in the air

I want to stand still forever

Paul Petrie

↶ THE INDOOR CAT

Hunts—through clear glass windows—
blue jays, chipmunks, mice.
Heaves up beneath curved palms
fur so softly sleek
the caressing hand delights.

Plays endlessly, preens
endlessly—on paws as pure
as milk eats from the kitchen
counter pellet-meat,

and hides from children's wars
under sofa caves and chairs,
ears slant and tail atwitch.

Kills nothing, fathers no one,
hones its claws
on the back of the red love-seat,

or sleeps, curled up in balls,
dreaming of hot pursuits
on running feet.

And shut, by chance, outdoors,
crouches under the leaves
of the rhododendron—trembling
at the shadows of wind and sun.

Is pampered, prospers, lives long,
has no fleas.

Jarold Ramsey

℘ COMET AND TREEFROG

What we've come for is the Comet,
  of course, and there in the northwest sky
over the dark woods sure enough it floats,
  more eerie than we'd heard, a luminous cloud,
a feather in the void, a sign
  from afar we hadn't thought to ask for.
In this mid-March twilight
  it is a wonder not to warm by.
Let the eyes have it. Meanwhile
  in the woods directly before us, the ears
have latched onto something—down in the mud
  one peeper, after his kind, is becoming millions,
shrilling their old din so insistently
  they will bring on the leaves and the birds
before we know it. Farewell, Comet Whatsyourname,
  we'll see you around.

ᴐ POWER QUEST, SOOKE PARK

Wind, surf, rock-cliff, sunlight—
all assault me on this treeless headland
where I crouch, no quarter given. The cries
of shearwaters and gulls tear
like rope through a rusty pulley,
hoisting me up to snap and belly
over the beaten kelp of my life.
This wild wind gives me back my true breath,
I live from exposure
to exposure.

Pattiann Rogers

∽ INTO THE LIGHT

There may be some places the sun
never reaches—into the stamen
of a prairie primrose bud burned
and withered before blooming,
or into the eyes of a fetal
lamb killed before born. I suppose
the sun could never shine by its own
light back beyond the moment
when it first congealed and ignited.

And Mohammed, it is said, never showed
the inside of his mouth.

But the sun is certainly present
in the black below the earth, shining
inside the surf and thriving minerals
of sycamore, beech and hickory roots.
Blind fishes at the perpetually sunless
sea bottom hold some daylight
in their bodies by the descending
crab particles and plankton crumbs
they sift through and swallow.

The sun of ten million years previous
stabs and glimmers still in the suspended
beat of glacial bacteria, dormant
and frozen beneath miles of ice,
And sun off sunflowers gone
for a hundred years is yet here today
in paint on canvas, just as the radiance

of summer trout watched by Schubert
is the sound of sun now in notes
printed on a staff.

And the sun may shine inside a rock
buried on the dark side of the moon,
if I imagine it there. It might illuminate
the buried night existing inside a dead
man's heart, if I say it is so.

If I envision it, could the sun,
shining maybe at first only faintly
like a penny candle or with a light dim
as the light of the Weaver Star, reveal
the outlines of descending salvation
in an icy rain falling at midnight
through a still forest, the black edges
of atonement in the wooden blades
of the desert saltbush? I close
my eyes and turn in that direction
to see.

ᛊ THE KINGDOM OF HEAVEN

inside of which careen
the wrecked suns of obliterating
stellar furies and smelting quasars
ejecting the seething matter of stars
in piercing shocks wrenching and spewing
the blasted flares and ash of incinerated
planets whose roaring eruptions
and scorching thunders, in the slightest
proximity, would boil and melt the ear
to spent char long before those sounds
could ever reach the ear as sound

inside of which exist
the serenities of this fading summer
evening, the motion of wind in slow,
shifting passions down from redcedar
and netleaf, across the easy flight
of creeks and bluegrasses, within
the peace of possibilities created
by a single cricket in his place,
the assurance of blindnesses behind
my eyes closed on this hillside,
earth pressing against my body

inside of which wheel
fine solar particles and microscopic
constellations issuing and collapsing,
waging transformations, gatherings
and dissolutions through bones and veins,
circling and spinning in pursuits and purposes
with bloody powers and strategies

inside of which is one
deity proven by the faith of sleep
and the imagination to exist throughout
these realms of such measured light
and destruction

Pattiann Rogers

✑ OPUS FROM SPACE

Almost everything I know is glad
to be born—not only the desert orangetip,
on the twist flower or tansy, shaking
birth moisture from its wings, but also the naked
warbler nestling, head wavering toward sky,
and the honey possum, the pygmy possum,
blind, hairless thimbles of forward,
press and part.

Almost everything I've seen pushes
toward the place of that state as if there were
no knowing any other—the violet crack
and seed-propelling shot of the witch hazel pod,
the philosophy implicit in the inside out
seed-thrust of the wood sorrel. All hairy
saltcedar seeds are single-minded
in their grasping of wind and spinning
for luck toward birth by water.

And I'm fairly shocked to consider
all the bludgeonings and batterings going on
continually, the head-rammings, wing-furors,
and beak-crackings fighting for release
inside gelatinous shells, leather shells,
calcium shells or rough, horny shells. Legs
and shoulders, knees and elbows flail likewise
against their womb walls everywhere, in pine
forest niches, seepage banks and boggy
prairies, among savannah grasses, on woven
mats and perfumed linen sheets.

Mad zealots, every one, even before
beginning they are dark dust-congealings
of pure frenzy to come into light

Almost everything I know rages to be born,
the obsession founding itself explicitly
in the coming bone harps and ladders,
the heart-thrusts, vessels and voices
of all those speeding with clear and total
fury toward this honor.

Reg Saner

∽ AUTUMN ASPENS: CUMBRES PASS

Though stands low on the mountain
remain green as sliced limes,
higher up, midsummer's far gone

in flaming amazement. When wind
riffling a ridgeline grove
fans our caveman sense of fire

as a wonder lovely to own,
over Cumbres Pass gold leaves
spill and spin like doubloons

till flame and coin seem one,
close as we'll come to money
on trees loved for their moment

almost better than money. Just when
have we spent such afternoons?
Less than once in a hundred?

That many? Then stop the car
again. At happiness to burn. Bright
as the life we're still looking for.

℘ CAMPING CLEAN

. . . comes easy as turning to look
at grasses your torso and shoulders
left flattened: where home
was one night, not more, and fires low
as blue roar from a tiny brass stove
since charcoal's more durable far
than we are. Camping clean's simple
as tent-sites left what they were,
natural as touch-and-go lightly,
till the hawk skimming daybreak
at the top of the sky can't tell,
nor will even those highest red ledges
yesterday's sundown slowly let go of
be able to say your hand climbing
past, then beyond them, was real.

✐ DESERT WISDOM

Across a red west of great mesas
gone blue there's nothing human to see

and I love it, love the whole desert's
wise way of saving room for the gods

surviving as exiles; powers so obscure
they may never have left, or gone far,

ones whose disguise has taken them ages
through the dim handful of the mind,

where earth's spirits must go to enter
changed names. Toad song, flax flower, agave,

salamander, datura. Gods forgotten as such
by all but the canyon's big-falling river

and moonrise over rimrock; thus humble
as even this twisted mesquite tree,

its precious few leaves, whisper-thin,
the night wind among them.

ᴄᵖ INDIAN PEAKS, COLORADO

Upheaval's stone garden
all around. The grand slabs
tumbled among each other's arms.

As along Indian Peaks
craglines darken to nothing
but a twilight of beautiful pain
I see creation begins
being endless up here: this last
paradise of first things.

Wind the only motion. My small fire
the final tree. And, looking up,
the star nations.

✐ MORNING SNOWFIELD

Where high-country evergreens grown taller
than drifts get wind-bitten clean as old bones,
and timberline fir crowd into windrows
thicker than cattle, knowing buried alive's
their only salvation, my snowshoes pause,
motionless as this weather's rare calm.

Light inside mountain cloud amasses, stalls,
then gently unravels, one casual close
that re-opens over glimpses of sky's teal blue.
As around me six-sided crystals prism or flare
with all the small colors of life, the low, slow
cumulus warps below summits. And fire

electromagnetic thrown raw off the sun
softens as it falls through straw-colored cloud
across snowy tundra. Falls as if it cared.
Over silence so vast; so visible, so absolute,
I've come to a standstill of joy, at home

just here, just now. As if I myself
were the world's first morning.

℘ RAIN NEAR HEART LAKE

Toward evening it ends. Day's overtures
close on the scent of wet conifers,
dusky droplets of glint. As pikas tweet,

their quick pinches of fur
trickle and dart over the time of rocks
while up higher, James Peak finally catches

through cloud its last chance at sunlight
so utterly clear all surface depth
opens. And how else but not trying

could everything here come with us?
Doesn't possession begin with admitting
we have none?—till what's real

grows apparitional. The goshawk's wing
then hangs on a sunset empty and generous
as the mind of heaven in motion

over Heart Lake, where this very light
and its mountain, twelve full seconds more,
stay alive undivided.

Forth from my literal door I'm greeted
by the sky gods—but not really; by spoken
reflections instead, orbiting lately
as "Jupiter," "Venus." Between hydrogen
fusion east, and its fires electromagnetic
off a westering moon, I'm a flick of reality
skewed—amid foothills of rock and wild
withered grasses browsed by a doe
with her still-spotted fawn. Blue mingle
of gases overhead. Planet-breath, fresh-lit
by the nearest star. If for eons pre-human
solar gold has indeed flung its great blaze
of evanescence, uninflected by even aerobic
bacteria, so what? And if dawn should prove
my best habit, it still mustn't presume
to be virtue. Just literal, and me-infested
and local, I know, just now. Just true.

∽ SIERRA CUP

To travel high summer
from the inside; to weight water
so heavy, so chill, so pristine, it's naked
as the summits it comes from; to plunge a hand
among boulders charging madly upstream;
to feel its handle yank at and flutter half free
of your fingers; to catch that dim chime
stainless steel barely gives off, nicking rock
underwater; to wet shirt-cotton with dribbles
so icy the frontal lobes ache like migraine
after each swallow; then, as that fades,
to dip again to the bottom of the world's well
which around here is snowpack so near to the sky
that's pretty much what it tastes like,
you could borrow this cup.

☞ THIS GRIZZLY

Is a plantigrade-gaited and prowly inquisitor,
an individual,
huge-humped and hulking, a sulker,
bilge-bellied, bossy-broad, is a boreal
and forest-fearsome crush of claws,
is claws alive
with bloom, with tundras of mud;
is hunger-hearted and ugly, a horrible beauty,
a hairy breath of berry-laced and blood-hot red,
hunter and hunted, and hated.

Is a greens-grazer
and grocer, a corm-cruncher, a salad-snatcher,
a riffle-raiding salmon smacker, an elk eater, a basher,
a mouse mauler, a moose muncher,
a maw.

And is furthermore female,
for males a mighty mountable smell and color,
and coupled is fecund: a cub-collared sponge,
a food-filter, a milk-mill—comfy for sucklings
but for all others
Big Mama,
one-fanged and angry fur-cloud brown.

This grizzly is poached, is paw-prized, applauded, appraised
as "impossible,"
is study-surrounded, rounded up and counted,
is sleep-shot and rifled, radio-rigged and revived,
is written down, written off, is wrangled over
under its own naturally brave and too-brazen nose

as if any such four-footed wilderness
might be, for what we've become,
just too mixed a blessing,
so meanwhile
thus hounded, thus parked, thus impounded,
encircled, bewildered and further endangered,
this grizzly is pondered.

If between basin and range you wake
at the middle of nowhere, its four
sacred mountains—north, south, east

and west, like cardinal points of morning,
may rise up as testaments that desert
isn't a bit sentimental. Though Utes

still consult them, and Paiutes and Zuni
and Hopi, their summits founded on days
of no eyes to go into (beyond table-top

buttes) seem so remote as to notice
only how wind gets such a lot done.
That's why when dawn's cirro-stratus

Unravels high as half of forever
its web of rose fire, and cloud-shadows
slide blue over red ruin in star-broken

sea floor, you waken from dreams facing
the sacred: a petroglyph only reason's
miracle opens. Inward as the pulse

of a wrist-vein, yet general as sunrise
declaring this riven middle of nowhere
and the hills of heaven one thing.

Susan Schaeffer

❧ THE DOG

There is everything in his eyes.
Everything.
Packs of wolves fleeing across the frozen waves,
Black shapes into the blacker woods
And he is there.
Once he was one of them.

Such muscles in his legs,
Such thighs,
Such hinged jaws. A giant of a dog
Who barks at horses, sheep,
Mistaking them for the wolf he still is.

Today he lies on the rug,
Tail bandaged, a giant, a walking house
Brought down by fleas.
And yet there are meadows in his eyes,
Steep, sharp cliffs toward which the sheep
Drift like suicidal clouds,
And as he dreams,
His muscles twitch,
In nightmares it is always the same,
He sees the danger, cannot raise his head,
Cannot bark nor move.

When he opens his eyes,
He takes it all in, what has become of him,
His people, whom he loves,
Moving through such familiar rooms,
The small cat who dances by,
These things are his to keep.

Is he diminished?
He thinks not.
He says, I have known love,
They touch my fur with love.
I have not sold my soul
For a safe haven, a handful of bones.

And yet, in dreams,
He is running free
And his people stream behind him
Like flags, like wind-tossed rags
Who will catch up with him
When he gets where he is going,
When he once more
Knows what he has always known.

Tom Sexton

∽ SEAL ISLAND

Across the meadow, sea smoke
rises from a cove,

distant islands float above
the icy bay,

this world seems about
to disappear,

and
how would we imagine

salt and seaweed, cedar
wet with rain?

❦ SKIMMING THE ICE

We talk of a friend
who is reading
everything he can find
on the coming millennium
as we walk to the stream
where we get our water.
No trace of the hole
we chopped two days ago,
so we take out our axe
and make another one,
blue-green ice darkening
the closer we get to the bottom.
When the axe breaks through
the hole begins to fill
and we rush to fill our jugs,
skimming new ice from the surface
before it freezes over,
water stinging our hands
as we work.
Back in the cabin,
you say that prophets seldom
come from cold places
and go about preparing supper.
The water boiling on the stove
smells of silverweed and sedge.

Peggy Shumaker

⌯ AJO LILY

Two feet deep
under quartz and silica

under earth no path
marks off

the bulbs swell,
sweetness too deep

to lure larvae,
ground too hard

even wet years
to tempt claws.

Impossibly delicate
one layered shoot reaches up

pushing aside
massive rubble

rearranging the mosaic
of surface pebbles

so these clear blue bells
might echo

ajo, ajo
the sky's voice

moments before
first drops bruise

dry earth,
before first drops

bead jojoba pods
where the swallowtail

drinks, moments before
a new shoot

slips slick as garlic
into a world deep blue

slit by sheet lightning,
pounded by hard water

insistent that we give
what we have

only ourselves
to feed all the world's hungry.

Joan I. Siegel

✌ DROUGHT

This is a season of holding back.
For forty days and forty nights
the sky will not give rain
and the earth hardens like a fist.
Even if the rain came
it would roll off the ground like beads of glass
and crack.

The air is mute
and dryness has its own sound
in the brittle grass
where hummingbirds search
the dusty mouths of day lilies.

At night
the milkweed explode
one by one
into the silence.

✑ How the Tortoise Knew It Was Her Time

Did the sun dip into the water this morning
staining it with blood, an omen
while the pale moon looked on like a blind eye
or is it how the water moved and didn't move
around the water lilies or the way the lichen spread
over the rocks or because of a sudden agitation
in the beating of the dragon flies' wings or how
the day lilies spread open and shut or something
in the blue of the Sweet Williams reminded her of winter
and loneliness edged downward from her belly
so that she heaved herself out of the pond
and up the steep roadside to dig the hole where she sits now
still and purposeful as if to say,
it suffices

℘ WILD HYACINTH

In the frozen ground under my feet
the wild hyacinth
neither patient nor impatient
curls up like a thought
before the words that name it.
And there it rests
until one warm afternoon in spring
when I have other things on my mind
it rises through the dead leaves.

John Smelcer

❧ BONANZA CREEK

Years ago I came here
after the lightning burn.
Now I come alone
in search of spruce hens
hidden in the tender growth.
I go deep
into your singed forest
of birch and spruce
whose roots once drank
from the blue waters
of the rainbow trout.
And resting on a burnt log
among lupin and larkspur,
I see in the ashes
beside the fireweed
a single wild rose.

My Indian Grandmother Speaks to Animals

For Morrie Secondchief

October & winter had begun.
Its long hair, white & braided
lay loose across a naked forest.
Grandmother came out
from her sagging cabin
which dragged the frozen earth
like a seine.
Among the last to speak our language,
she came & stood beside me
as I measured grizzly tracks
in crushed snow with the sole of my shoe.
Just then two tundra swans passed,
white as the hills & sleek.
They called down to us.
Grandma turned her face to the sky,
told me in our words,
Nalt'uuy ggok xonahang—
"They're telling us good-bye."
We watched them disappear
into thin-curved horizon,
announcing their leaving
to those who would hear.

Nunyae Senk´aaze

—from the Ahtna Athabaskan

Da´atnae nii sii nunyae senk´aaze
ghayaał tic´aa ikae daa.

Sii niic tah sii ciił
yuuł deniigi
naan hwzaak´e
k´e deniigi nak´
yii dzaadze´ tic´aa
ts´abaeli´ eł k´ey—

sii nake´taen hnax gha tene
´eł´aen sk´e
yii k´adiidi sesi.

Animal Spirits

Old men teach me animal spirits
wander the forests where they once lived.

I remember as a boy
chasing a moose
across a frozen field
until it vanished
in a tangled forest
of spruce and birch—

how I turned home on our trail
and found only my tracks
in the fresh crushed snow.

Katherine Soniat

℘ DOG DAYS

From the window
I watch the blue containment of noon,

and every day the dog trots into it,
pees sprightly on the clover,

then makes headway through the timothy grass,
his coat full of seed. Perhaps

he has some idea of what wants him
and where to go, and since he's no skeptic,

he goes—rye, corn, the whole fermenting
season ablaze, the dog running off

as if to make August history.
Who's to say

his is not the same lithe world
that swayed before pharaoh's daughter

and the baby in the bulrushes.
And this sun overhead

heated the earth when voices flared
a final, frantic time

for Joan on her pyre of wood.
Timely, these moments

of lives waiting in reeds
or balancing atop the sticks,

while the dog, he flops down
after a day of futile adventure,

the ravine glistening with wings
and an undergrowth of eyes.

Michael Spence

♗ THE FIG CURTAIN OF ATHERTON

—Queensland, Australia 1986

In a land named
For a queen, life kneels only
To older royalties. The eucalyptus—
Bark in shreds
As if flayed by the wind—
Pulls a kukkaburra out of the sky.
The bird drops
The seed of a fig tree
Among the top branches. Sending roots
Thin as vines
Down the trunk, the seed
Erects a stalk. Before the fig can reach
Soil or sky,
Something—wind, disease,
A sudden shift of the earth—fells the tree
Against another.
The fig keeps growing roots: a fibrous curtain
That will not part.
Generations of sloths
And koalas climb the ropes of wood.
At last the leaning
Eucalyptus dies,
Rotting away. In the world, what reigns
Is what survives.
The wind, with majesty,
Flows through it, trying to make a harp
Of this gnarled ribcage.

Matthew J. Spireng

∽ SNOWY OWL

Even here, thousands of miles
south of where it hatched,
it adapts for a while,
flashing at night from rooftop
to steeple and frightening
drunks who think an angel's
come to carry them home.
Ledges are cleared of pigeons
as it sates its hunger.
A stray dog finds heaven
in its bony cast.

William Stafford

ᴄᴘ Gulls at Cannon Beach

You'd think they discovered injustice and achieved
a new righteousness. They turn on their storm-earned
voices and come in on the arc of their wings
for today's caucus, take a pose, walk pigeon-toed
a few steps, measure their neighbors for size
and gravity. Then they stand on one leg for hours
and think about things, like how far it is
to Alaska, and what island offers best nesting.
Conservative, well dressed and deliberate,
sometimes they lift all at once, test the wind
and prove with a flourish of feathers Isaac Newton
all over again. They circle awhile, blaming this place
unanimously and considering choices next time,
maybe Tolovana, or even Neskowin.

Martin Steingesser

Open the windows.
Everyone in the house is happier. The house
is happier, fresh air
in our mouths—finally. Purple finches
sing on the telephone wire, one finch singing
out his scarlet brains. Everyone
is happier, even the chair
beside the window, the cat
in the chair more possessed of the moment
than Buddha. All the windows are open,
coffee is up, and you laugh, pointing—
"The groundhog's out!"

Dabney Stuart

∽ Where the Deer Go

Uprearing from the thrashed
snow—first the classic head
poised on the neck, flexed, eyes
unpuzzling, then the rest
of the body
unshambling, flank
and thigh, foreleg
and hoof, the red bloom
closing behind the erect
shoulder—the whole
unstinted creature
lifts from its strung
suspension above the snow
bed as if to rise
weightless across the rim
of cedars.
        Released, it passes
the bead, moves backward
along the barrel,
through the corrected
sight into the hunter's
eye, his mind
a covert of mast and stillness
where the hammer
never falls, his forefinger
tapping lightly against
the trigger guard
another dance
altogether.

Brian Swann

✐ FLYING FROM THE CENTER

We are flying from the center/
multiplying as we burn.
                    —W. S. Merwin

The cold front's pressed the eastern sky
brighter and brighter till it
goes out in a burst of no color.
The wind rivets the cranefly
to the pane, bends his legs like
a demented dancer frozen in space.

I am at my desk, waiting for the rain
and reading about madness.
Someone is talking about nice things,
how one should concentrate
on the pleasant experiences, go for
long walks by the sea, listen to the birds.

But suddenly there are no birds.
And in the silence, rain is a wrong
done us all. On my blank pad
I complain: the past will not deliver
the future again. I'm surprized to discover
I mean what I say.

↝ THE LAND AT THE WORLD'S END

There's something uncertain about the rock
at my feet. Moss covers it,
soft in a way gales make it, and black squalls.
Someone came to the village. He said,
I'd like to know if you fear death
in those small boats. I fear the man
who asks me if I fear death.

Hours I've sat here
watching the sea squirm in a nor' wester
that almost takes my head off.
In this glassy light, persistent as if
a torch shining from beneath
meets another just above the surface,
the red tips of the moss glow
like tiny matches against the gale's rasp.

Elf-shots in the fields, fossil
Footprints, standing stones, the Brannocks
leading out to sea . . . And we are squeezed
into this land at the world's end.
The birds go quiet about now,
knowing something they can't tell,
something like colors to a blind man.
You see them hunkered on rocks
like old shipwrecked sailors
talking about something they don't want
to remember.

⌒ OLD SONG OF THE MUSK OX PEOPLE

It is glorious
when the caribou herds leave the forests
and begin to wander northwards.
They are on the alert for deep pitfalls in the snow,
the great herds from the forests, when they spread
   out over the snow—
they are glorious!
It is glorious
when early summer's thin-coated caribou begin to wander;
When at Haningassoq, down there, over the promontories,
they mill back and forth looking for a crossing place.
It is glorious
when the great musk oxen
down there, glossy, black,
cluster in small groups
to face and watch the dogs.
When they bunch together like that
they are glorious!
The women down there are glorious
when they go visiting the houses in small flocks,
and the men down there suddenly feel
the need to boast and prove their manhood,
while the women try to catch them in a lie!
It is glorious
when the winter caribou with their thick coats
begin their trek back, in toward the forests.
They are glorious!
They look about anxiously for people.
When they are moving in towards the forests
they are glorious!

The enormous herds are glorious
when they begin to wander down there by the sea,
down by the beach.
The creaking whisper of hooves when they begin
    to wander around—
oh, it is glorious!

From a song transcribed by Knud Rasmussen
in Intellectual Culture of the Copper Eskimos, *1932*

‌ WALKING AT NIGHT

I open the top
of my door & stand
in the dark
blue rush of air.
Hold my breath
to know what breathing is.
Air will move through me
as it moves through the trees.
I push open the bottom.
The path has not yet
been mined in the melt.
There is time.
In the hemlocks I can still
hear the silence owls
made, though the stream
clashes about. I am
walking. Snow reflects
blank sky. I feel my eyes wide
as shoulders. Now I am young.

Roberta Swann

ᴄᴘ EFT

Two days' rain. The minute it stops, I'm out.
Everything is lit. The landscape's an enclosed universe.
Blackberries dangle. I eat so many so fast
my belly aches. A deer has just crossed. As I bend
to heart-shaped tracks, I'm surprised by a flame-
orange eft, so tiny, yet jurassic. Lifting each tentative leg,
it takes my heart away.

I walk up the path. Mist rises off mountains,
a moving still-life. A squirrel skydives
down a maple alarming a chipmunk who chirps
a warning that wakes a woodchuck who waddles
off like a big girl in a small sweater.

Suddenly all's right with the world.
I can't wait to say so. Zooming downhill,
I skid to a stop. My eft is dead,
lying in a fetal position, a speck of orange leg
inches from its baby face, that even lifeless
looks like it was born too soon.

Joan Swift

ᡈ ANTHURIUMS, PAHOA

Exhilarating, something I can't explain,
their effect on me those days in Pahoa

when at the edge of the sea blue was too much
and, besides, I was a stranger on an island.

They liked to crowd together in buckets, touch
each other all over abundantly, show a

gift for togetherness whenever my eyes found
them in dim garages. Their eruption

from the arms of an old Japanese
woman crossing the street was better than volcanic,

leaving nothing of darkness behind. I was
alone but they never were, repeating red

from their own tubers, a trick
that led them wild through the whole ohia forest,

runaway colts that chose to be blessed,
nuzzling that closeness in the rain I wanted.

ᘓ STEELHEAD IN THE WHITEHORSE REARING POND

As if they don't always remember that twining,
dorsal to pectoral fins, braiding of glides,
like that silver pair I watched in a clear
cold stream where they danced their lost pavan.
As if they've forgotten once there were still
transparent eddies along the river for such
potentials, glassy reflections of cedars,
milt drifting like snow in a natural watery pasture.
As if they don't see we've come with our
chainsaws and mudslides, fishing rods,
trawlers and gillnets, dams for light
to read our greedy history by. As if they don't
know this pond has concrete walls like any prison,
that they never again can be wild but only
swim out through a culvert or two
returning by memory, odd and almost saved.

WILD SALMON: STILLAGUAMISH TRIBAL HATCHERY

for Levi

He wades in neoprene boots the tank's
fake eddies, swirling his net and missing
and swirling for the heft of her belly, its
yield. She's ready, no river's
split reflections for disguise like those
under Oso bridge where Fisheries took her.
She was already dying. You can tell
he loves her the way he tenderly
slits her flesh for eggs,
their weight in the swinging tin
all the past, the future of her kind.
Then it's time to slash the male,
pour its milt in the yellow bucket
with her eggs. These metal trays,
disinfectant, labels, a stream
through pipes into fiberglass troughs—
what else can he do not to lose them?
They were always fierce in the old days.
Their leaps unravelled the rival stars.

David Wagoner

ᴥ MAKING CAMP

You've found the place in time—no permanent shade,
A level path between your feet and water,
And luck for kindling,
So you drop your pack and begin staying alive
Through the coming night. You haven't indulged yourself
Too long on the trail
To watch the sunlight changing clay and sandstone
To bastions and castle keeps, to vaults of fool's gold,
So you see your way
Clear to the vital stage of rest and shelter.
A man on a journey must be a journeyman.
You make your campfire
First on bare ground (all stones near water are full
To bursting) with a backlog at least as long
As you are tall, a companion
Whose substance will comfort you as it turns to ashes.
Now you may eat whatever seems edible,
And since your weather
For a while to come isn't dropping anything
Unbearable on you from the evening sky,
You may lie down
By the fire and try to think yourself asleep
Or to think of nothing but sleep or to think hard
Of nothing at all,
Because if you intervene in the open-ended
Discourse between the earth and heaven, the rock
And the hard place, whose discord
Resounds and reverberates in every imaginable
Direction *and* its opposite, the vibrant
Crosstalk of earthlings and godlings,

Their babbling and chuckling, moonflies, star-bait, the streakers
Across the belts from Van Allen to Orion,
You'll bring your mysteries
To light again and croak yourself awake
Like the frog in your throat announcing your survival
To the chorus of morning.

R. and T. Weiss

ᢒ   THE LOST WOOD

Our old neighbor,
an ornithologist, kept
that little wood. Last
stand it was of sycamore
and locust from the forest
which once swept across
the land.
        Kept here mid-
town to ensure the birds,
opossums, flocks of deer
their browsing rights,
unharried tenantry.

And for our sakes kept
to keep some portion
of this country's past:
each dawn accompanied,
each feathery dusk,
with trills echoing
among the wood-winds,
every breeze inspired.

The old man dying,
deer and birds alone
attended on this wood,
the element, and—some
warble luring—you and I.

Then one early dawn
screeches tore the sky.
Before the day was done
the wood had disappeared.

While the winds hiss
through, a moan of tongues
plucked out, a lone blue
jay, fixed on a stump
like a moment's monument,
looks and looks on all
the toppled, empty scene.

Little that it sings,
complains, bewildered
it must be, bewildered
past the reach of pain.

Nancy Willard

℘ SAND SHARK

Sealed in your pewter coat,
your belly white
as a starched cuff,
you died in the tracks

drawn by your dorsal fin
as you heaved at low tide
toward pages of water
turning and turning.

I could read by the light
that pours from your sockets.
Picked clean, they open
on boney chambers crammed

with roses that darken
behind your nostrils,
finely drawn on the rounded
cone of your nose, like

needle holes left
by stitches so small
even your breath
couldn't find them.

CONTRIBUTORS

ANTLER, from Milwaukee, is the author of *Factory* (City Lights), *Last Words* (Ballantine), *Ever-Expanding Wilderness*, and *Deathrattle vs. Comecries*. He has won the Walt Whitman Award and the Pushcart Prize. For the past twenty-five years he has spent a month or more alone every fall backpacking in the wilderness.

ALISON APOTHEKER teaches creative writing and literature at Portland Community College in Portland, Oregon. A recipient of an Oregon Literary Arts fellowship, she has published poems in *Prairie Schooner, Alaska Quarterly Review,* and *Permafrost,* among others.

HOMERO ARIDJIS has published twenty-seven books of poetry and prose. Two collections of poetry have appeared in English: *Blue Spaces* and *Exaltation of Light,* and three novels: *Persephone* (1985), *1492: The Life and Times of Juan Cabezó of Castile* (1991), and *The Lord of the Last Days: Visions of the Year 1000* (1995). In 1987 he received the Global 500 Award from the United Nations Environment Program on behalf of the Group of 100, an environmentalist association of writers, artists, and scientists, of which he is founder and president.

DENISE Y. ARNOLD, a British cultural anthropologist, works with Aymara-speakers in highland Bolivia; she writes and teaches in London and Latin America. Her publications include *Hacia un orden andino de las cosas* (1992), *Madre Melliza y sus crías, antología de la papa* (1996), and *Río de vellón, río de canto. Cantar a los animales, una poética andina de la creación* (1998), with Juan de Dios Yapita.

ROBIN BECKER, associate professor of English and women's studies at Pennsylvania State University, will publish *The Horse Fair,* her fifth collection of poems, in spring 2000 with the University of Pittsburgh Press. Her *All-American Girl* (University of Pittsburgh Press, 1996) won the 1997 Lambda Literary Award in Lesbian Poetry.

TED BENTTINEN is a poet living in Rhode Island.

BRUCE BERGER's essay collection *The Telling Distance* (University of Arizona Press, 1990) won the 1990 Western States Book Award. Subsequent books include *Almost an Island*, a personal narrative of Baja California (University of Arizona Press, 1998), and a poetry collection, *Facing the Music* (Confluence Press, 1996).

WENDELL BERRY is the author of more than thirty books, including essays, novels, and poetry. He has received numerous awards, including the T. S. Eliot Award, the John Hay Award, the Lyndhurst Prize, and the Aiken-Taylor Award for Poetry from the *Sewanee Review*. His most recent books include *A Timbered Choir: The Sabbath Poems 1979–1997* and *Selected Poems of Wendell Berry*.

JAMES BERTOLINO won the international *Quarterly Review of Literature* Book Award for his eighth full-length collection of poems, *Snail River*, published in 1995 by the *QRL* Poetry Series at Princeton University. Lately he has been a visiting professor teaching literature and creative writing at Willamette University in Salem, Oregon.

SALLIE BINGHAM is a writer whose novels and memoir have been published by Houghton Mifflin, Viking Press, Knopf, and Zoland Boooks. Her poetry has appeared in the *American Voice, Connecticut Review,* and *New Letters*. She lives in Santa Fe.

STEVEN BLEVINS was a long-time staff member at the Natural Resources Defense Council, as well as a poet and an artist. His creations include luminous and startlingly original collages, in addition to drawings and hand-crafted cards. He was also a prolific and talented writer, as the poetry published here attests. He died in 1994.

PHILIP BOOTH is well into his eightieth decade. His recent tenth book from Viking is a millennial *New and Selected: 1950–1999*, in all its many meanings.

ROBERT BRINGHURST was born in 1946 and has lived for many years on the coast of British Columbia. There he writes both poetry and prose and translates from Haida and other Native North American languages. His books include *The Calling: Selected Poems, 1970–1995* (McClelland and Stewart, 1995), and *A Story as Sharp as a Knife: The Classical Haida Mythtellers and Their World*.

JOSEPH BRUCHAC is a writer and storyteller who belongs to the Abenaki Indian Nation. His newest books include *The Trail of Tears* (Random House, 1999) and *No Borders*, a poetry collection from Holy Cow Press (1999).

HAYDEN CARRUTH lives in upstate New York. He has published forty-one books, chiefly on poetry, but also prose fiction, criticism, and two anthologies.

ROBIN S. CHAPMAN's poetry has appeared recently in the *Hudson Review* and *Southern Review*. *The Way In* (Tebot Back Press, 1999) is her third collection of poetry; *Banff Dreaming* (Firewood Press) is a recent poetry CD. She lives in Madison, Wisconsin.

PETER COOLEY was born in Detroit and grew up there and in the suburbs of the city. He is a graduate of Shimer College, the University of Chicago, and the creative writing program at the University of Iowa. Since 1975 he has taught creative writing at Tulane University. His six books include *The Company of Strangers, The Room Where Summer Ends, Nightseasons, The Van Gogh Notebook, The Astonished Hours,* and *Sacred Conversations.*

W. S. DI PIERO is the author of numerous volumes of poetry, prose, and translation. He lives in San Francisco and teaches at Stanford University.

SHARON DOLIN's collection of poems, *Heart Work*, was published by the Sheep Meadow Press in 1995. She is also the author of two chapbooks: *Mistakes* (Poetry New York Pamphlet Series, 1999) and *Climbing Mount Sinai* (Dim Gray Bar Press, 1996). She has taught literature at the Cooper Union and creative writing at the New School and the 92nd Street Y in New York City.

MICHAEL DORRIS's many books of fiction, nonfiction, and essays include *Broken Cord*, for which he received the National Book Award in 1989, *Yellow Raft in Blue Water* (1987), and *The Crown of Columbus* (with Louise Erdrich). Part Modoc, he was professor of anthropology and Native American studies at Dartmouth. He took his own life at age 52 in 1997.

CONSTANCE EGEMO received an R.N. from Hamline University in St. Paul and then attended the University of Minnesota, where she studied with poet Michael Dennis Browne. Her first book of poetry, *Dreams and Silences*, was recently issued by Blue Light Press in Iowa.

RICHARD ELMAN wrote more than twenty-five books. A collection of his poetry will be published by Junction Press. *Namedropping: Mostly Literary Memoirs* (SUNY Press) is now available in paperback. His translations of *Phoenician Women* (Euripides) and *The Girl of Samos* (Menander) are published by the University of Pennsylvania Press (1998). His novel *Tar Beach* is available from Sun & Moon Press. He died in 1997.

CHARLES FISHMAN served as director of the SUNY Farmingdale Visiting Writers Program for eighteen years. His books include *Mortal Companions* (1977), *The Firewalkers* (1996), *Blood to Remember: American Poets on the Holocaust* (1991), and *The Death Mazurka* (1989). Fishman currently serves as poetry editor for both *Gaia* (www.whistle.org) and *Cistercian Studies Quarterly*. He is the winner of the 1999 Eve of St. Agnes Award from *Negative Capability* and served as final judge for the 1998 Writer's Voice Capricorn Book Award.

BRENDAN GALVIN's recent books are *The Strength of a Named Thing* (1999) and *Sky and Island Light* (1997), both from Louisiana State University Press, and the narrative poem *Hotel Malabar* (Universityof Iowa Press, 1998), winner of the 1997 Iowa Poetry Prize. He lives in Truro, Massasschusetts.

KENNETH GANGEMI has three books of fiction in print: *Olt, The Interceptor Pilot*, and *The Volcanoes from Puebla*. He lives in New York City, where he is working on a novel and a second collection of poetry.

FAYE GEORGE grew up in Weymouth, Massachusetts, where the woods and ponds of her Iron Hill Street neighborhood imprinted her with an enduring love of the natural world. Her poems have appeared in *Poetry* and other periodicals and anthologies. She now lives in Bridgewater, Massachusetts.

EAMON GRENNAN is an Irish citizen who has lived in this country for over thirty years. His books include *What Light There Is and Other Poems, As If It Matters, So It Goes,* and *Relations: New and Selected Poems*. His volume of translations, *Leopardi: Selected Poems*, won the 1997 PEN Award for Poetry in Translation. He teaches at Vassar College.

AIMÉE GRUNBERGER (1954–1998), a lifelong poet, published three chapbooks in her furious last years: *Ten Degrees Cooler Inside Dead, Hope for the Wrong Thing,* and *He Spoke to Maria*. An honors graduate of Brown University, she was twice a finalist for the Walt Whitman Poetry Prize and taught poetics at the Naropa Institute's Summer Writing Program.

JOHN HAINES is the author of numerous collections of poems and critical essays, most recently *Fables and Distances: New and Selected Essays; The Owl in the Mask of the Dreamer: Collected Poems;* and *The Stars, The Snow, The Fire*. He is the recipient of fellowships from the Guggenheim Foundation, the National Endowment for the Arts, and the Academy of American Poets, and in 1995 received a literary award from the American Academy of Arts and Letters. He homesteaded in Alaska for more than a decade, and currently resides in Montana.

BRIAN HENRY's first book of poetry, *Astronaut*, appeared in the United Kingdom in late 1999. His poems have appeared in numerous magazines around the world, including the *Yale Review, American Poetry Review*, and the *Paris Review*. He is an editor of Verse.

WILLIAM HEYEN's books include *Pterodactyl Rose: Poems of Ecology; Crazy Horse in Stillness*, winner of the 1997 Small Press Book Award for Poetry; and *Pig Notes and Dumb Music: Prose on Poetry*, which contains several ecology-related essays. He is professor of English and poet-in-residence at SUNY Brockport.

PATRICIA HOOPER is the author of two books of poetry, most recently *At the Corner of the Eye* (Michigan State University Press, 1997). Her poems have appeared in the *American Scholar, Atlantic Monthly, Poetry, Kenyon Review*, and other magazines. She was awarded the Norma Farber First Book Award of the Poetry Society of America in 1985.

BEN HOWARD's books include *The Pressed Melodeon: Essays on Modern Irish Writing* (Story Line, 1996), *Lenten Anniversaries: Poems 1982–1989* (Cummington, 1990), and *Midcentury* (Salmon, 1997). A recipient of a National Endowment for the Arts fellowship, he is a frequent contributor to *Poetry, Shenandoah, Sewanee Review*, and *Amicus*. He teaches literature, writing, and classical guitar at Alfred University in upstate New York.

CORAL HULL is a poet living in Australia.

DAVID IGNATOW is the author of eighteen volumes of poetry and three books of prose. In a career spanning more than fifty years, he received the Bollingen Prize, two Guggenheim fellowships, the Wallace Stevens fellowship from Yale University, the Rockefeller Foundation fellowship, the Shelley Memorial, the award from the National Institute of Arts and Letters "for a lifetime of creative effort," the Robert Frost Award, the John Steinbeck Award, and the William Carlos Williams Award. He died at his home in East Hampton in 1997 at the age of 83.

MARK IRWIN is the author of four collections of poetry: *The Halo of Desire; Against the Meanwhile; Quick, Now, Always: Poems;* and most recently, *White City*, published by BOA Editions in 1999. He has also translated two volumes of poetry. He is currently a visiting writer at the University of Colorado at Boulder. He spends part of each year on a wilderness ranch in south-central Colorado.

GEORGE KEITHLEY's poems, stories, and essays have appeared in the *New*

York Times, Harper's, Kenyon Review, TriQuarterly, Agni, and Sewanee Review. His award-winning epic, The Donner Party, a Book-of-the-Month Club selection, has been adapted as a stage play and an opera. He lives in northern California.

MAURICE KENNY, recipient of the American Book Award, has authored, among other works, Tekonwatonti: Molly Brant; On Second Thought; and Backward to Forward (essays). He lives in the Adirondack mountains.

URSULA K. LE GUIN, born in California in 1929, lives in Oregon. She has received many academic, popular, and literary awards for her more than forty books of fiction, poetry, criticism, and children's stories. Her most recent books are a translation of Lao Tzu's Tao Te Ching and a collection of recent poems, Sixty Odd.

DENISE LEVERTOV published more than twenty volumes of poetry between 1946 and her death in December 1997. She also wrote essays, edited a number of books, and translated three works of poetry. Her final volumes include New & Selected Essays (1992); Sands of the Well (1996); and This Great Unknowing: Last Poems (1999). The Letters of Denise Levertov and William Carlos Williams was published in 1998. She taught for many years at Stanford University, and was the recipient of numerous awards, including a Guggenheim Fellowship, a National Institute of Arts and Letters grant, the Lenore Marshall Prize, and the Lannan Award.

WILLIAM MATTHEWS died in November 1997, shortly after his fifty-fifth birthday. His final collection of poetry, After All: Last Poems, was published in 1998.

JAMES C. McCULLAGH is a poet living in Pennsylvania.

CARRINGTON McDUFFIE is a poet living in California.

GEORGE McWHIRTER was born in 1939 and educated at Queen's University, Belfast. His awards include the Commonwealth Poetry Prize, the Ethel Wilson Prize for Fiction, the F. R. Scott Prize for Translation, and the LCP's Canadian Chapbook Competition. He teaches poetry, fiction, and literary translation at the University of British Columbia.

ROGER MITCHELL is the author of six books of poetry, most recently The Word for Everything (1996) and Braid (1997). His book of nonfiction, Clear Pond: The Reconstruction of a Life, appeared in 1997. He lives part of the year in Bloomington, Indiana, and part in Jay, New York.

GARY PAUL NABHAN is director of conservation and science at Arizona-Sonora Desert Museum and author of fourteen books, including *Cultures of Habitat.*

DUANE NIATUM was born in Seattle, Washington, and has spent most of his life in that evergreen city. He writes essays on contemporary American Indian art and literature, but he is better known for his poems and stories. *The Crooked Beak of Love*, his sixth volume of poems, is forthcoming from West End Press. He is about to complete sixteen stories based upon his Klallam people's myths and legends.

JOHN O'BRIEN lives in West Virginia. His work has appeared in *Hudson Review, Iowa Review, Massachusetts Review, TriQuarterly, Gray's Sporting Journal, Country Journal,* and other journals. He is currently working on a memoir, *At Home in the Heart of Appalachia,* for Knopf.

MARY OLIVER is the author of twelve books of poetry. She received the 1993 Pulitzer Prize for *American Primitive* and the 1992 National Book Award for *New and Selected Poems.* She is also the author of *A Poetry Handbook.* Her most recent publication, *Winter Hours,* is a collection of poetry, prose, and essays. She teaches at Bennington College in Vermont.

SIMON J. ORTIZ grew up in the Acoma Pueblo in New Mexico. He has published numerous volumes of prose, short fiction, and poetry. His most recent works include *Woven Stone* (1992); *After and Before the Lightning* (1994); and *Men on the Moon: Collected Short Stories* (1999).

JOHN PECK recently published his *Collected Shorter Poems* with Northwestern University Press (1999).

JIM PETERSON's collections of poetry are *The Man Who Grew Silent, Carvings on a Prayer Tree,* and *An Afternoon with K.* Poems have appeared in *Poetry, Georgia Review, Poetry Northwest, Prairie Schooner,* and *Antioch Review,* and other journals. He is coordinator of creative writing at Randolph-Macon Woman's College in Lynchburg, Virginia.

PAUL PETRIE has published eight books and four hundred poems in eighty-two magazines, including the *Atlantic, New Yorker, New Republic, Hudson Review,* and *Poetry.*

JAROLD RAMSEY grew up on a ranch in central Oregon and has taught for many years at the University of Rochester. His books of poems include *Love in an Earthquake, Dermographia,* and *Hand-Shadows,* which won a

Quarterly Review International Poetry Prize. His work on American Indian literature includes *Reading the Fire.*

PATTIANN ROGERS's two most recent books are *Eating Bread and Honey* (1997) and *The Dream of the Marsh Wren: Writing as Reciprocal Creation* (1999) both from Milkweed Editions. *Collected and New Poems, 1981–2001* will also be published by Milkweed. She is the recipient of two NEA grants, a Guggenheim fellowship, and a Lannan Literary Award.

REG SANER is the recipient of the Wallace Stegner Award from the Center for the American West; his poetry and prose have won numerous honors. Saner's *Reaching Keet Seel: Ruin's Echo and the Anasazi* (University of Utah Press, 1997) features setting, sites, and ancient cultures of the Southwest.

SUSAN FROMBERG SCHAEFFER is the author of nineteen books, five of them collections of poetry. Her latest novel, *The Autobiography of Foudini M. Cat,* was published by Knopf in the fall of 1998 and has been translated into many languages.

TOM SEXTON is Alaska's poet laureate. His poems have appeared in the *Hudson Review, Paris Review, Poetry,* and other collections. His latest book is *Leaving for a Year* (Adastra).

PEGGY SHUMAKER was the 1999 poet-in-residence at the Stadler Center for Poetry at Bucknell University. Her most recent book is *Wings Moist from the Other World* (Pitt Poetry Series). She and her husband live in Fairbanks, Alaska, and travel widely.

JOAN I. SIEGEL's poetry has appeared most recently in the *American Scholar, Commonweal, Yankee, Nightsun, Amicus, New Letters,* and other journals. Her work is anthologized in *American Visions* and *Beyond Lament.* She is the 1998 recipient of the Anna Davidson Rosenberg Award.

JOHN E. SMELCER's recent poetry books include *Songs from an Outcast* (with an introduction by Denise Levertov and X. J. Kennedy) and *The Snow Has No Voice.* He is poetry editor at *Rosebud.*

KATHERINE SONIAT's third collection, *A Shared Life,* won the Iowa Poetry Prize. Her work has appeared in *Poetry, TriQuarterly, Amicus, Southern Review, Appalachia,* and *ThreePenny Review,* among others. She is on the faculty at Virginia Tech.

MICHAEL SPENCE drives a public transit bus in Seattle. His poems have appeared in *American Scholar, Georgia Review, Poetry, Poetry Northwest,* and *Sewanee Review.* His second book is *Adam Chooses* (Rose Alley Press, 1998).

MATTHEW J. SPIRENG is the assistant city editor for the *Kingston (N.Y.) Daily Freeman,* and holds an M.A. in creative writing from Hollins College. *Out of Body,* a collection of his poems, was a finalist for the 1998 Cleveland State University Poetry Center Prize.

WILLIAM STAFFORD was the author of thirty-five books and recipient of several major awards, including the National Book Award for *Traveling Through the Dark.* He was a lifelong teacher who shared his thoughts with countless students through his thirty years as professor of English at Lewis and Clark College in Portland, Oregon. Stafford was born in Hutchinson, Kansas, in 1914; he was named the Oregon Poet Laureate in 1975, and died in 1993.

MARTIN STEINGESSER performs his poems and stories in a diversity of styles and was winner of the first two poetry slams at the Maine Festival of the Arts (1992 and 1993). His poems have been published in the *American Poetry Review, American Voice, Beloit Poetry Journal,* and the op-ed page of the *New York Times.* His story *The Wildman,* with woodcuts by Vermont artist Mary Azarian, is available from North Country Press. He works actively in the artist-in-residence programs of the Maine Arts Commission.

DABNEY STUART has published fourteen books of poetry, fiction, and criticism, most recently *Long Gone: Poems* (Louisiana State University Press, 1996) and *The Way to Cobbs Creek* (stories, University of Missouri Press, 1997). A new volume of poems, *Settlers,* is forthcoming from LSU Press. A former Guggenheim Fellow in Poetry and NEA Literary Fellow (twice), he lives in Lexington, Virginia.

BRIAN SWANN has been poetry editor at *Amicus* almost from its inception. He has published a number of books, including poetry, short fiction, children's books, and translations, and has edited volumes on Native American literature. He teaches at the Cooper Union.

ROBERTA SWANN is a cofounder of the American Jazz Orchestra and was director of public programs at the Cooper Union. Her writing has appeared in *American Voice, North American Review, Kenyon Review, Crazyhorse,* and other magazines.

JOAN SWIFT's fourth full-length book of poems, *The Tiger Iris*, was published by BOA Editions in the fall of 1999. She is the author of three other books of poems as well as a chapbook, *Intricate Moves: Poems About Rape* (Chicory Blue Press, 1997). She is the recipient of three NEA creative writing fellowships.

DAVID WAGONER's *Traveling Light: Collected and New Poems*, was published in the summer of 1999 by the University of Illinois Press. He edits *Poetry Northwest* for the University of Washington.

R. and T. WEISS have published the *Quarterly Review* for over fifty years. They recently received a PEN Club Special Achievement Award, and T. was given the Oscar Williams/Gene Derwood Prize for his poetry. R. and T. are finishing a book of poems they have written together.

NANCY WILLARD's recent books include *Swimming Lessons: New and Selected Poems* (Knopf); an anthology, *Step Lightly: Poems for the Journey* (Harcourt); and *Cracked Corn and Snow Ice Cream: A Family Almanac* (Harcourt). She teaches in the English department at Vassar College.